PRAISE FOR SEXPERIMENT

"Ed and Lisa Young have modeled a Christ-centered marriage for over twenty-five years. Their straightforward, encouraging, and practical teaching in SEXPERIMENT will take your marriage to a greater depth of intimacy than you've ever known before."

—Craig and Amy Groeschel, senior pastors, LifeChurch.tv;
author, *WEIRD, Because Normal Isn't Working*

"Honestly, most of the preaching and teaching about sex, love, and marriage is not getting the job done. The marriages and sex lives represented in the church look no better than the world's. And the reason is because our approach to the subject is based on restraint rather than vision. In SEXPERIMENT, Ed Young, a man with a marriage and family worth aspiring to, changes that. If you want to experience all of the pleasure and happiness God intended for your marriage, this book is a must-read."

—Steven and Holly Furtick, lead pastors, Elevation Church;
author, *Sun Stand Still*

"Ed and Lisa Young are longtime friends of ours, both personally and in ministry. Their sense of humor, love for life and for growing a church full of flourishing Kingdom-minded people is contagious! They care deeply about people and their marriages; and offer a perspective that makes this book a good read!"

—Brian and Bobbie Houston, founding pastors,
Hillsong Australia

"Ed and Lisa are simply fun to be around and their joy as a family speaks even louder than their world-renowned church does. My wife and I look at their marriage, the way they still laugh with each other and live life so passionately, and are instantly inspired. Additionally, all their children actually want to hang out with them! Higher praise for parents you will not find. Obviously, their marriage is impacting, if it works in their own house first. This book should be a premarriage prerequisite and an annual 'wanna stay happily married' reread! Thank God for a couple that continues to help others build strong marriages."

—Carl and Laura Lentz, lead pastors,
Hillsong NYC

"Marriage without good sex is like a house without heat in the winter. You might be able to survive in it but it's not nearly as enjoyable. Ed and Lisa are among the best when it comes to encouraging us to keep the "heat on" in the house. Their practical, honest, and open style of communication on this topic is both real and refreshing. We encourage you to take this challenge as an opportunity to stir the fire in your marriage."

—Kevin and Sheila Gerald, pastors,
Champions Centre

"Our culture worships sex but is often confused about marriage. I've always believed that the church should be at the forefront in portraying the delight of sex in the context of marriage. Ed Young's book does just that with humor, wisdom, and candor."

—Judah and Chelsea Smith, senior pastors,
The City Church

"It's not a lack of love that makes a marriage monotonous; it's a lack of passion. SEXPERIMENT will help you put the passion back where it belongs . . . and take your marriage where it needs to be!"

—Rev. Run

SEXPERIMENT

Days to
Lasting Intimacy with
Your Spouse

ED AND LISA YOUNG

New York • Boston • Nashville

All Scripture quotations, unless otherwise noted, are taken from *The Holy Bible, New International Version* (North American Edition), copyright © 1973, 1978, 1984 by the International Bible Society. Used by permission of Zondervan Publishing House.

Scripture quotations noted NKJV are taken from *The Holy Bible, New King James Version*, copyright © 1982 by Thomas Nelson, Inc. Used by permission. All rights reserved.

Scriptures noted NLT are taken from *Holy Bible. New Living Translation* copyright © 1996, 2004 by Tyndale Charitable Trust. Used by permission of Tyndale House Publishers, Inc., Wheaton, Illinois 60189.

Scripture quotations marked *The Message* are taken from *The Message*. Copyright © 1993, 1994, 1995, 1996, 2000, 2001, 2002 by NavPress Publishing Group. Used by permission.

Scriptures noted NASB are taken from the *NEW AMERICAN STANDARD BIBLE®*, Copyright © 1960, 1962, 1963, 1968, 1971, 1972, 1973, 1975, 1977, 1995 by The Lockman Foundation. Used by permission.

Scriptures noted NRSV are taken from *New Revised Standard Version Bible*, copyright © 1989 National Council of the Churches of Christ in the United States of America. Used by permission. All rights reserved.

FaithWords
Hachette Book Group
237 Park Avenue
New York, NY 10017

www.faithwords.com

Printed in the United States of America

RRD-C

Originally published in hardcover by Hachette Book Group.

First trade edition: January 2013

10 9 8 7 6 5 4 3 2 1

FaithWords is a division of Hachette Book Group, Inc.

The FaithWords name and logo are trademarks of Hachette Book Group, Inc.

The Hachette Speakers Bureau provides a wide range of authors for speaking events. To find out more, go to www.hachettespeakersbureau.com or call (866) 376-6591.

The publisher is not responsible for websites (or their content) that are not owned by the publisher.

The Library of Congress has cataloged the hardcover edition as follows:

Young, H. Edwin, 1936–
　　Sexperiment : 7 days to lasting intimacy with your spouse / Ed and Lisa Young.
　　　p. cm.
　　ISBN 978-0-446-58272-8
　　1. Sex in marriage—Religious aspects—Christianity.　2. Intimacy (Psychology)—Religious aspects—Christianity.　3. Sex—Religious aspects—Christianity.　I. Young, Lisa.　II. Title.
　　BV4596.M3Y68 2012
　　248.8'44—dc23

ISBN 978-0-446-58271-1 (pbk.)

2011038117

CONTENTS

We want to dedicate this book to everyone who understands the reality that great marriages don't just happen; they take work. It is through a commitment to one another, a passion for each other and a willingness to work together that husband and wife experience true joy in marriage and fulfillment of a lifelong journey together.

ACKNOWLEDGMENTS

When we began to write this book, we knew that it would be a tremendous undertaking—one that would require the assistance, guidance, and support of many other people. No author sits down from beginning to end and does it all alone. Like marriage, writing a book takes the work and dedication of more than one person. We want to recognize some of those who played key roles in helping this book become what it is.

First and foremost, we thank God for creating us as relational beings and blessing us with the opportunity to share His message for marriage.

To Tom Winters and Debby Boyd, we appreciate your guidance and connection on so many fronts. Tom, Something like this is not possible without someone like you in our corner.

To Jana Burson and all those at Hachette Book Group, thank you for the opportunity to work with you on this project.

To Olivia Cloud and Andy Boyd, thank you for your dedication and assistance in helping us compose, write, and edit this book.

A huge thank-you to everyone who submitted their stories of how the Sexperiment helped their marriages and improved their lives. Your willingness to share provides another dimension for everyone who reads this book.

And finally, our deepest appreciation goes out to the great people of Fellowship Church, whom we first challenged with the Sexperiment. It is an honor to be able to open God's Word and share with you each week all that He has in store for marriage, relationships, and life.

SEXPERIMENT

INTRODUCTION

When I was four years old, I asked my mother the question that every child wants to know at some point: Where do babies come from? Since I am the oldest of three boys, this was the first time my mom had faced this question, and her reaction was understandably shock and stall.

But I've never been content with asking a question once and not getting an answer. I'll keep pursuing the answer until I'm satisfied that I have received *all* the information I need. So I didn't just ask my mom once. Or twice. Over and over (and over and over), I bugged her to tell me where babies come from. I asked in grocery stores. I asked in church. I asked at the dinner table. I asked all the time. And my mom knew that unless she answered me honestly and completely, I would simply keep on asking.

Finally, after eluding the subject several times, my mom realized I wasn't going to stop asking, so she sat me down to give me the answer. In the most age-appropriate way she could, she explained to me the intricacies and terms of pregnancy. And because you can't talk about where babies come from without broaching the subject of sex, she explained "it" in very broad terms.

When she got done dispensing as much information as she felt was appropriate for a four-year-old boy to have, I sat there and let it marinate in my mind. After a few minutes, I looked up at her with a straight face and simply said, "I don't believe you. **Who in the world would want to do *any* of that?**"

Now, more than forty-six years later, twenty-nine of which I've been married, I can say, "Mom, I believe you. And I now know why anyone would want to do that!"

Sex. For such a small word, it has an enormous influence on our lives. From the time we're very young, sex is something we hear about, talk about, and think about—whether it's in a healthy way or not. It's in our music. It's in our movies, television programs, magazines, and books. Conventional wisdom in the advertising industry is "sex sells." If they want to sell a product, from shampoo to automobiles, they do all they can to get us to believe it will make us be more sexy, or get more sex. Yet, no matter what we may think we know about sex, so many people don't understand the full effect it was designed to have.

The Sexperiment is a challenge that was created to help you and your spouse reconnect with what sex is supposed to be. The premise of the challenge is simple and clear: Have sex with your spouse once a day for seven consecutive days. It may not seem like a lot on its surface, but the implications of having sex for a week, as you will discover in reading this book, are much more intricate and will produce long-lasting results. For one week of your life, if you decide to take it on and get it on, the Sexperiment is designed to help you realize just how much sexual intimacy can do for your marriage.

But why seven days? Why not fourteen or ten or even three? After all, you may be thinking, "We haven't even had three straight days of sex since we first got married. I'd settle for that!"

There is something special about the number seven. There are seven days in the week. There are the Seven Wonders of the World. God even made the world in seven days. In the Bible, the number seven often symbolizes wholeness or completion.

But let's be real. None of us is creating a new world. We aren't marking off a map of the greatest architectural achievements of humankind. We aren't looking to restructure the modern-day calendar. But we are striving for wholeness and full satisfaction in marriage. The Sexperiment can be the first step.

So the next question is, can having sex for a week really make that much of a difference in my marriage? Is it really that big of a deal in the overall picture of my marriage and my life? The answer, Lisa and I believe, and based on our personal experience, is yes!

How the Sexperiment Started

The catalyst that sparked the idea for the first Sexperiment came from my wife, Lisa. I was in the middle of a teaching series about the dangers of lust and she handed me an article from a parenting magazine about the sex lives of couples with children. As I scanned the article, the research was depressing. It basically said that couples want to make love, but the reality is that they don't do it nearly as much as they'd like.

As I flipped through the magazine, I came across another article about a couple that had committed to having sex at least once a day for an entire week. They called it a "Sexperiment," and they shared some of the challenges that the week presented, along with many phenomenal results it brought into their marriage.

As I read those two articles, I thought, "This is something that could help so many couples today. And the best place to talk about this is in the church!" So the following weekend, at the nudging of my wife, I challenged the husbands and wives of Fellowship Church to have sex for the next seven days.

As was expected, the men cheered and most of the women looked at me with incredulity. But after several days, the e-mails and calls flooded in from wives and husbands alike, thanking me for encouraging them to take the challenge!

Ed,

I thank God for you and your wife! Thank you for finally teaching us the truth! My husband and I are on day nine, so that should tell you something, LOL.

Thank you, thank you! This seven-day sex challenge, Ed, is golden! Showers of praise from my wife and I, whose sex life over the years has stagnated and become, I suppose, a little rusty.

We have a ritual now, my wife and I: after dinner, sit by our fire and share a cup of tea, bagging our usual TV indulgences in favor of talking and sharing our days, which leads not only to emotional intimacy but, now with your challenge, a desire to turn that back into physical intimacy as well.

Challenge Rules

Before we go any further, I want to make something very clear. The Sexperiment isn't for everyone. It's reserved for those who are married, because God designed sex to be enjoyed within the marriage bed. He created it as something sacred to be shared between a husband and wife in the context of marriage.

For too long, though, people of faith have danced around the subject of sex and allowed culture to hijack God's design for it. Now, sex is everywhere, even where it shouldn't be. Our world is surrounded and compounded by the implications and ramifications of "doing it" the wrong way. But the fallout of sex out of context is something that the entertainment industry, advertisers, marketers, and sales reps don't like to talk about.

It's not that we don't think about sex. That's a natural part of being human. The problem is that we don't think deeply enough about it.

Many sexually active people don't understand what sex is really all about. They are convinced that sex is just a physical routine, a biological act between two people. They believe they can separate the physical act of intercourse from its relational, emotional, and even spiritual repercussions. But that is impossible.

Maybe you are a Christ-follower. Maybe you consider yourself to be a spiritual person. Or maybe you don't believe in God, the Bible, or the church. No matter where you find yourself spiritually, I encourage you to continue reading. Because as you get into the pages of this book, you'll begin to see sex in a way you never have before. You'll see it as so much more than a physical act. It is a gift from God that is emotional, physical, psychological, and above all, spiritual.

In the minds of most people, the only time sex and God should intersect is in a single exclamation of ecstasy: "Oh my God!" Sex has become just sex. But while society has taken sex too far, the church hasn't taken it far enough. We've got to take this gift back and use it in a God-given way, which is within the context of marriage, the ultimate goal being a lifelong commitment.

Christians tend to think that sensuality is carnality, but in actuality it's spirituality. We've kicked the bed out of church and God out of the bed. We need to bring the bed back in the church and God back in the bed. In studying the Scriptures, I see the obvious connection with God and sex. God is all about unconditional love—connecting with us—and that relationship is illustrated in the act of marriage.

In this book, we're reconnecting sex with God and God with sex. I want married couples to read this book and have great sex. That's the goal because God is a great God who creates great things, like sex. For years as a pastor, speaker, and author, I have worked to communicate that sex is a beautiful thing, because it comes from God. Somewhere along the way, that message has been lost, but that is going to change.

What Seven Days of Sex Can Do

Do you have great sex with your spouse? As you embark on the Sexperiment, you'll begin to see some reasons why you may not be having the kind of sex life you want. If you're having pretty good sex in your marriage, the Sexperiment can help you and your spouse move from good to great in the bedroom.

Maybe you're wondering how having sex for seven days in a row can affect the present state of your marriage. You may be thinking, "We had sex every day when we first got married, but it didn't really do anything for our marriage."

But think about it. Usually newlyweds are more considerate of each other, more attentive to each other, and more concerned about how to please each other. I believe that frequent sex plays a part in that.

As you do the Sexperiment, you and your spouse are going to have sex for seven days with a purpose—greater intimacy with each other and, ultimately, greater intimacy with God. The challenge is about recapturing some of what may have been lost as you began to have sex less frequently.

As newlyweds, you didn't have to think about intentional intimacy. You felt close all the time. Intimacy—physical, emotional, or otherwise—was second nature to your relationship. This time, as you and your spouse have sex for seven days, you'll be surprised what it will reveal about your marriage. There's a lot of stuff—deep stuff—going on in people's lives, and maybe in your marriage, too. There may be pain, mistrust, or betrayal involved. If this describes the state of your marriage, the Sexperiment can be the catalyst that begins to unpack feelings and emotions that have long been buried. In this week of intentional sex, you will move toward a place of true intimacy and openness.

What does intimacy mean? It means to be *fully known*. Intimacy is a good thing. So in marriage we're to be intimate in every way—physically and emotionally and economically and psychologically and spiritually. The Sexperiment will set you on a path toward greater intimacy by making sex a priority for one full week, and hopefully beyond.

Is intimacy between you and your spouse a priority in your marriage, or do you only make love whenever you get around to it? The Sexperiment will show you where you stand.

When people accept a challenge, they "step up." So I challenge you to take the Sexperiment and bring your best game to the bedroom. This exercise will make your marriage better. Hundreds of couples have taken up the gauntlet, and the results have been tremendous, and not just at Fellowship Church!

> I heard about this challenge in the news...I was laughing so loud because I didn't think I could make it. My husband and I now have five non-stop days and we are very close, we are happier, and every day we thank the Lord for our blessings. As a married couple we are better and we can't live without each other.

Change Your Sex, Change Your Marriage

I'm not saying that a single week of whoopee will change your marriage forever. That's an ongoing process that takes time and intentionality. What I am saying, though, is that the Sexperiment will give you a foundation to build on. It will cause you to reconnect because it challenges you to bring your best game to the marital equation.

Here's the point: What happens outside the bedroom affects what happens inside the bedroom. And what happens inside the bedroom affects what happens outside the bedroom. By having more sex, you will change what goes on outside your bedroom, which is where the bulk of marriage takes place. Don't be shocked, but sex is a mental thing long before it's a genital thing. It's between your ears long before it's ever between your legs.

The truth is, sex is multifaceted and multidimensional. The complex components that make up sex can't be taken apart or rearranged any easier than you or I could take apart and rearrange the seasons of the year. And as you read this book and take this challenge with your spouse, you'll discover just how many of those aspects play a role in all other areas of your marriage.

By now, you may have one more question before reading any further: "What is a pastor doing writing a book about sex? What does he know?" Well, Lisa and I have learned a lot through our own marriage, but I've also learned a lot from counseling hundreds of married couples. I've seen firsthand the collateral damage that accrues when one or both spouses choose to sleep in the wrong bed. Sleeping in the wrong bed is costly—physically, emotionally, and relationally. It is so much wiser and better to protect this deepest level of intimacy by keeping it within the guidelines and guardrails of marriage.

The Sexperiment will take you on a journey that can save you from that kind of devastation and heartache. Even if your marriage has been damaged by infidelity, abuse, or neglect, doing the Sexperiment can help you rebuild intimacy in your marriage and experience ecstasy like never before.

The Sexperiment can help you whether you've been married for thirty years, like Lisa and me, or if you've been married three years, whether you're about to be married or you don't see a marriage prospect for miles. **Everyone needs to know the truth behind God's design for sex.**

If you're on the road to building an intimate relationship with your future mate, this book can help you understand the complex union called marriage and help you understand what it really takes to make your marriage successful. "Before You Do" is a special section at the end of each chapter designed to encourage engaged couples to work on identifying potential barriers to intimacy in marriage.

It's never too early in your relationship to get on the right track for intimacy in marriage, and it starts with having your mind, body, and spirit ready to receive the right mate. Being unequally yoked is the first building block for a disastrous marriage, and if you're single you want to prayerfully take every precaution to keep this from happening to you. "The Yoke Is Not a Joke" will guide single read-ers through the Sexperiment material as you prepare yourself to be marriage-ready. As you wait for God to provide the right mate, you don't want to settle for just a bed partner. Sex is an important and sacred part of marriage, and when a couple is equally yoked, it can be their most beautiful and meaningful expression of love.*

The Sexperiment puts sex back where it belongs, in a place that is sacred, beautiful, and God honoring. When we glorify God as we have sex, we're taking sex, and marriage, to an HNL—a 'hole 'nutha level—a divine level!

This book is about sex, but not about sex techniques. It's not a manual. This book is about understanding sex the way it is intended by God to be—between a man and a woman in the context of marriage. The Sexperiment is about what sex is and what it isn't. It's about making a priority and about making love. By making sex a priority for seven days, it will challenge you to communicate about technique with your spouse and bring creativity into the bedroom. And as you do, you'll discover (or rediscover) the joy of connecting with your spouse regularly, even in the midst of a NASCAR-paced life.

Sex should never be the sole foundation for any relationship (Christ should occupy that position). But once you are married, the sex you share can play a major role in upholding the rest of your relationship. As any architect, CEO, or head coach will tell you, a fantastic foundation is critical for a solid structure to withstand the external and internal pressures it is bound to face. It's true with buildings, businesses, and sports teams. It's true with marriages as well.

That's exactly what the Sexperiment can help you achieve—a solid foundation upon which you can build (or perhaps rebuild) a

---

* The term "yoked" comes from the Bible and is simply a farming reference. When a farmer would plow a field, he would use a yoke to join two animals. The goal was always a straight line in the field, so the farmer would pair animals of equal strength. When it comes to marriage, God challenges Christians to "yoke" themselves to other like-minded believers. It's a pipe dream to think two people of polar opposite spiritual beliefs can plow a straight path for their marriage or their children in the future. It's just not going to work. But when two people of equal strength join in marriage, the result is amazing.

better, stronger, more lasting, and enjoyable marriage. And *that's* what this challenge is all about.

It's about what sex is. It's about what sex represents. It's about what sex can do for you—physically, relationally, and spiritually.

Now, husbands and wives—get ready to take the challenge of your (sex) life!

1

Seven Days of Sex

♡

Think back to the early days of your marriage. You and your spouse were loving, considerate, thoughtful, and sexy—all the things that made you and your spouse want to be together. You made love a lot more often than you do now, too. But then some things happened. A demanding job, taking up new interests and hobbies and, later, kids can all drive a wedge between you and your spouse and block your attempts at retaining intimacy in your marriage. Slowly, complacency creeps in and sensuality seeps out.

As you clock some years in your marriage, so often a dual resignation takes place. If you have kids, the wife often steps down from her number-one position as the wife and becomes primarily Mom, often juggling a career with the responsibilities of raising children. At the same time the husband steps down from his primary position as the husband. As the woman shifts her focus to the kids, the man concentrates on his vocation.

While this shifting is going on, you become less of a couple and more like two people who just share the same address. You're gradually moving in opposite directions. She starts reading romance novels or *Cosmo*, wishing her marriage could be as wonderful as those articles promise. Meanwhile, he may start surfing for Internet porn or watching *Girls Gone Wild* commercials and fantasizing about a life that includes lots of sex without all the hassles. Then throw an attractive coworker or neighbor into the mix, add a few dashes of fatigue, and a sprinkle of humdrum, and you've got a recipe for an "unsuccesexful" marriage that lacks true intimacy or a deep bond. All you need is a lawyer to put it in the oven and turn up the heat. This process happens slowly and methodically in marriage after marriage.

This is the stage at which many modern couples divorce. Half of all first marriages in the United States end in divorce, even among Christians. Even if you manage to stay together, you may end up like so many couples who simply limp along in marriage.

That's not what God intended for marriage. Couples, Christian or not, face lots of challenges today that require them to make a conscious decision to fight for their marriage.

Modern marriages seem to fall victim to a lie that the world communicates: "Hopefully you'll have a few good years, if you're lucky. But don't be surprised when complacency sets in." Sadly, many marriages succumb to this lie, or worse ones, and end up in relational wreckage. The sad part is, it's the kids who really get hurt. Even adult children are hurt when their parents divorce.

It's time to reverse that curse.

Reverse the Curse

The Sexperiment can be the catalyst to reverse this curse and set you on a course toward greatness—toward true intimacy and fulfillment in marriage, the way God intended. He's the designer.

God wrote the manual for marriage. So if you want your marriage to change, go back to the manual. True change only comes from God, and we begin to change when we admit that we can't do it alone, but God can!

Maybe you're thinking, "Ed, I know something needs to be done to improve our marriage, but I just don't feel like I have the power to make it happen."

Maybe you're feeling that way right now because of the state of your relationship. Your marriage needs some work—maybe a little or maybe a whole lot—and you don't think there's anything you can do about it.

Maybe you're thinking, "But you don't know what's gone on in our marriage. It's pretty bad."

In most cases, no matter how bad the circumstances—hurt, betrayal, boredom, complacency—a dead marriage can be resurrected, and sex can play a big role.

Maybe you find that hard to believe, but it's true.

Making love more often with your spouse can be the catalyst to resurrecting your marriage because God is at the center. During the Sexperiment, we're going to reconnect those words to help you and your spouse find your way to a great marriage.

Still not convinced that this challenge will help?

Think about it. God and sex are inseparable. After all, it was his idea. When Adam and Eve made love for the first time in the Garden of Eden, they didn't run behind some bushes and then emerge and say, "Hey, God! Guess what we just did? It was pretty incredible!"

And God didn't say to them, "Amazing! How did you figure that out! You mean the parts fit together perfectly? I had no idea!"

It didn't happen that way. Sex began in heaven. God thought it up. Our God is pro-sex and pro-marriage. He gave us sex primarily for pleasure, and secondarily for procreation. God made love so we can make love in marriage. He's the designer.

Every time we think about sex, we should think about God. Because if it's done the way God intended, it's truly an act of worship. And if we treat sex as an act of worship to God, we're thinking right. Because the way we think determines the way we feel; the way we feel determines the way we act. As I said, sex is between the ears before it's between the legs. So we've got to make the connection between sex and the designer, and discover the power to do something phenomenal!

People like wearing designer labels because they represent style and quality that is a cut above the common and ordinary. An ordinary marriage in our culture today is likely to end in divorce or continue in never-ending mediocrity. You don't want common or ordinary in your marriage. The Sexperiment will help you find your way out of mediocrity to marriage God-style.

Bridging the Gap

Sex, healthy sex, can revolutionize marriages. That shouldn't be a shocking statement. It's not counterintuitive. Yet, how many marriages are really doing it—and enjoying it—the way God intended?

In a *New York Times* article, couples were asked what they would most likely do on a Saturday night once the children are asleep. Thirty-eight percent of women and thirty-three percent of men answered "sleep."* Yet, at the same time, a *Los Angeles Times* article reported that "boosting the frequency of sex in a marriage from once a month to once a week brings as much happiness as an extra $50,000 a year."† Maybe that's the difference between NYC and L.A., but I think it's much deeper than that!

To put these stats another way, couples want to have more sex and think it would strengthen their marriage, but there is a shortfall, a deficit, a delta between wanting and having. The Sexperiment will put couples on the way to bridging that gap.

The gap doesn't appear overnight. It's a methodical process that many, many couples endure over years of a monotonous relationship. (Notice I didn't say monogamous relationship.)

This challenge will help reverse or avoid the predictable path of marital monotony. And it will guide you and your spouse onto a course of true intimacy. It's a process of creativity and change. Just so you know, it's not going to happen overnight (and the complete change won't happen even over the course of seven nights).

---

* http://parenting.blogs.nytimes.com/2008/11/25/time-for-parent-sex/?apage=2
† http://articles.latimes.com/2006/jul/03/local/me-happy3

Change is never easy, and true change comes from God. It's only when we begin to do things God's way that we can begin to take hold of the change He has in store for us. Your week of intentional intimacy will jump-start that change process for your marriage. It's like a shot of marital espresso!

So if you're ready to wake up, if you're ready to get your marriage out of the gap, it's time to step up and take the challenge.

Maybe you're thinking, "Sex for seven days? Too easy, Ed! I thought you said this was a challenge." Let me caution you. It's one thing to have sex for a week while you're on some tropical vacation island with no kids and no schedule to keep. It's another thing entirely to commit to doing it when you're also trying to do everything else your life requires—balancing your career, shuffling the kids to school and soccer practice, cooking meals, doing laundry, and overcoming the barriers that everyday life presents.

This challenge will require a definite commitment from the two of you to do it God's way for seven days. Some of you may think it's going to be easy, but by now I'm sure many of you recognize that fitting seven days of sex into your routine is going to take considerable effort. In the end, though, it will be well worth the effort and sacrifice!

Right now, you may not even see how seven days of sex can make a difference in your marriage, but it can. It's not such a stretch if you really think about it. Intimacy that is intentional and purposeful is going to shine a light on your marriage. That light will illuminate the positive aspects of your marriage partnership, but it will also give light to the more difficult places that have been unexposed and unexplored in your relationship. And it will show you just what you need to do to grow closer together as a couple.

What's Your Marital Work Ethic (MWE)?

"Wow, Ed, seven days of sex sounds like fun, but you're talking about putting in some work."

You're right! Marriage takes work. Marriage is not the easiest thing you will ever do, and it very well may be the hardest thing. But it can become the greatest and most rewarding, fulfilling thing when you do the work!

How hard are you willing to work to save your marriage, or even to have a better marriage? What would you do to regain the spark of desire and intimacy you once had? Do you give more than is required, or do you sit back and wait to see how much your spouse is willing to do before you decide to act? Do you approach your marriage thinking about what you can give, or is your concern only about what you can get?

I'm not going to pull any punches. Having a better, more fulfilling marriage takes time and effort, but the work is worth it! Here's what's so paradoxical. Maybe you've told yourself that it's going to take too much work to turn your marriage around. Well, if you were to decide to have an affair because it seems easier than working on your marriage, you have to work at that, too. Having an affair requires creativity, planning, sacrifice, time, money, energy, and intimacy! You can save yourself, your marriage, and your family a lot of heartache by committing to do the same kind of work with your spouse. In the process, you'll build a great marriage and leave a great legacy while saving yourself and others a boatload of pain and problems!

Put your best work into the most important earthly relationship known to humanity—marriage. Think about your job. You get up, have coffee, shower and get dressed to look as good as you can, and rush to the office so you can be on time. When you get there, you're making calls, you're taking initiative, you're contributing ideas in staff meetings, you're pitching innovations to this person and that person, you're bagging clients and you're doing the stuff that helps you be successful so you can keep your job. That's work.

What if you took that same level of energy and effort and put it into your marriage? Have you ever thought about what would happen if you treated your office or your work site like you treat your home? You can't show up for work in your underwear saying, "Where's the remote, honey?" That wouldn't work. We have to work to earn a living and we have to work to have a good marriage. It takes work to have a regular date night. It takes work to spend quality time talking and communicating with your spouse. It takes creativity to keep your marriage interesting. It takes effort to live out the marriage the way God designed it.

I remember officiating a wedding years ago for two bodybuilders. These exercise enthusiasts were standing there dwarfing me, and I went through the vows and the ring exchange. Then I said, "Now I want you to light the unity candle." So the bride and groom turned and grabbed their respective candles. For some reason, though, they got stuck in the candelabra. So, the big groom said, "Honey, excuse me," and she kind of backed away. I'll never forget this. He grabbed both candle stems and bent them in toward the center to light the unity candle!

Talk about becoming one flesh! But those bodybuilders taught me a lesson that day. A great marriage takes a lot of strength. It takes a lot of work, a lot of bending. That's the MWE—the marital work ethic—in operation.

Lisa and I have a high MWE, so we have a good marriage. I can tell you with complete confidence that we have a stronger love today than we did when we first fell in love more than thirty years ago. But we still have to work at our marriage. For more than a quarter century we have worked at our marriage. And believe me, there have been many times when we haven't felt like it, but we keep at it. We're very, very intentional about it. We've gone through dry seasons. We've gone through seasons when we were on a roll. We've gone through all of that. But even with all that we've been through, we're still motivated to keep working to make our marriage better. It's because we recognize the reality that God wants the best for our marriage, and nothing will stand in the way of that!

We're a busy couple. Between the ministry and the kids and the other demands of any married couple, Lisa and I have to work hard to maintain our MWE. We work harder to have a date night today than we did ten years ago because our lives are much busier. We have to work harder to carve time out for us to take trips together alone. But I'm going to tell you something. Every sacrifice, every trip, everything we've done has been worth it.

When you see or feel that marital drift happening—and it will happen—you've got to step up and step out to take the initiative and ride the crest of creativity. That's the time to reevaluate your MWE, because if you are not careful, your romantic pursuit of your spouse can lead to predictability. There's a certain level of comfort that can come from predictability, but at the same time it can be a marriage killer—predictability, monotony, and then throw in a couple of kids. Revolve your lives around the career and the kids and you know what happens after that, and it's not pretty.

Your marriage is worth the work that it takes to get your relationship to the level that God intended. Think of the Sexperiment as an enjoyable "workweek" to help you get to that place in marriage. Seven days of sexual intimacy reveals to you the labor of love you have to involve yourself in if you're going to reap the true rewards of marriage.

God is a God who works. In Genesis 1, God saw the results of his creative work and declared it all good. God made sex. God made marriage. And it's all good.

Church Says "Don't." God Says "Do."

Every time I speak on this fascinating topic, people hang on every word. Very few people fall asleep in church when I talk about sex!

Traditionally, when the church has addressed the issue of sex, it has tended to emphasize only negative aspects, the don'ts—adultery, homosexuality, promiscuity. It's always about the don'ts. All single people hear is "Don't do it until you're married." All married people hear is "Don't do it with anybody else." There is so much more to sexual intimacy within marriage than the don'ts!

For far too long, the church has neglected to teach the great side of sex, which God designed to be exhilarating, adventuresome, and fun. Good sex, the best sex, is biblical sex—one man and one woman within the context of marriage. We shouldn't be ashamed to talk about what God was not ashamed to create.

While the church has been largely silent, society has been very vocal about sex. It's everywhere, but most of what we get is misinformation. Some people listen to psychologists and doctors on television and radio talking about sex. Wives and husbands may take their sexual cues from magazines like *Cosmopolitan* or *Playboy*. They may buy products they've seen on TV that promise to bring back vitality and excitement to the bedroom. Other couples, in an effort to regain the spark in their marriage, may run out and buy a sex manual that resembles a *Popular Mechanics* magazine.

What would you say if I told you that the greatest sex manual ever written is probably already in your home. Maybe even on the living-room coffee table. Wait, before you start telling me, "No way, Ed. We don't allow that kind of smut in our home," just keep reading.

The greatest sex manual ever written is the Bible—the infallible, relevant word of God. In the Bible, God has set aside one book that shows how husbands and wives should make love. The Song of Songs (or the Song of Solomon) is a book within the Bible that shows how a couple can and should have sexual fulfillment in marriage. Now, before you make a mad dash to get your dusty Bible off the coffee table, let me share a few things with you.

Sexcellence in Marriage

The primary purpose of the Sexperiment is to help you in your quest for "sexcellence" in marriage, which leads to greater intimacy. And we can see that kind of relationship in Song of Songs.

Here's the context of the love story in Song of Songs: Solomon was the second son born to King David and Bathsheba. He was probably a good-looking guy, because his father was ruggedly handsome and his mother was drop-dead gorgeous. After David died and Solomon became king of Israel, he married a Shulamite woman. She and Solomon knew what it meant to really have love and intimacy in every slice of their marriage. Throughout Song of Songs, he and his wife talk about their courtship, their marriage, their problems, and how they handle those problems.

Solomon's defining legacy is that he was the wisest man who ever lived, and the Song of Songs offers a great deal of his wisdom about sexual fulfillment in marriage.

Maybe you can't imagine anything hot and steamy could ever be found in the Bible. Well, Solomon and his wife can probably teach you a few things and help enhance your marriage.

Now, let's look at this biblical couple with a hot marriage to learn something about what it means to have sexcellence in marriage, God's style.

A Succesexful Husband

Husbands, if your goal is to have a "succsexful" marriage, know that the first element is *Do the unexpected*. Let me explain what I'm talking about. One of the greatest needs a woman has is the R-word: romance. *"Ro Mance...Didn't he used to play for the Dallas Cowboys?"* No, no, men. Romance. Women love to be romantic. They love affection. And *you* have to set the stage and create the atmosphere for sexuality. As the leader of the relationship, men have to set the tone. Men have to understand what the word *romance* means.

Here's a biblical example of romance from Song of Solomon. In the first chapter, Solomon told his wife, "Our bed is verdant."* That word *verdant* means "covered with plants." Solomon did something totally unexpected and covered their bed with flowers. He said, "Baby, look at the bedroom." He set the mood. He was romantic. He built his wife a house and didn't tell her what the bedroom was going

---

* Song of Solomon 1:16–17

to look like. He paneled the bedroom with cedar. That's doing the unexpected.

When was the last time you did something romantic that was totally unexpected by your wife? When was the last time you purchased her a long-stemmed rose and just walked in—for no reason and with no ulterior motive—gave it to her, and said, "Honey, I love you"? Doing the unexpected will take you a long way during the Sexperiment.

My personal challenge, as far as the romance side of me goes, is that I get repetitive. I confess that I'm a guy who still messes up sometimes, even after thirty years. Guys are systematic: We do the same old, same old. Same restaurants, same waiter, same food, same movie, same babysitter, same lovemaking. Here's a tip: Anything that is repetitive, men, is a romance killer. One more time: Anything that is repetitive is a romance killer. If you're a woman reading this right now, you're probably nodding your head.

Give the Solomon technique a try during your week of challenge. Then, after you do the unexpected, do a second thing: *Take the initiative.* Again, we are talking about romance. Guys, romance needs to be the atmosphere in the home, and sex is the event. So take the initiative.

Think back to when you were dating your bride. When you thought about a date, who set the plans? You probably did it. You thought about the movie, you thought about the restaurant, you would call in advance and make everything work, you would think about what you would wear. You were planning and you were romancing her and you were dating her. Then you got married and started doing what I sometimes still do. I'll just get the paper and say, "Hey, Lisa, here's the paper. If we go to the movies, is there anything you want to see?" Or, "Let's just go to our favorite restaurant. In fact, they have a great special if we get there before five p.m...."

No, no, no, guys. That does not work when you're trying to build romance! Here's something else we do: We romance a woman and we really get into it; then we get married and we start acting like that task is complete, because men are task oriented. After marriage, we take our romance uniform off and it's like we retire it. We mount it on the wall with the wedding photos and say, "Hey, honey, remember that outfit right there? That was the uniform I wore when I romanced you. But we're married now, so who needs it?" Sound familiar?

Solomon—a wise husband—had it going on in the romance department. He told his wife, "Arise, my darling, my beautiful one, and come with me." He took the initiative. He dated his mate.

Men, you have to date your mate like you did before she was your wife. What you used to get her is what you still need to use to keep her. And I am not talking about double-dating! Double-dating went out with the junior-senior prom. It's wonderful to have couples to hang out with, but when you double-date, you and the other guy end up talking about sports while the women talk to each other about the clearance sale at Macy's.

Your marriage relationship, the one-on-one interaction, must take priority over any other, except your relationship with Jesus Christ. That's why I recommend that you go on a date with your spouse once a week, or at least once every two weeks.

It doesn't matter what you do. It doesn't need to be expensive or expansive. But you do need to do *something*. And you, husband, must take the initiative.

Third, husbands, *be impractical*. I am not making this up; this is biblical stuff. I looked up the word *impractical* in *Roget's Thesaurus*. You know what another word for impractical is? *Romantic*. Isn't that something? I know we have to be practical in life—stay within the budget, have reasonable expectations for progress, consider the needs of the children, and so forth. But if you're always practical, it's a romance killer. I am not talking about going out and getting into debt or something. Solomon said this: "Come, my lover, and let us go to the countryside. Let us spend the night in the villages." And this word *villages* in Hebrew means a bed and breakfast...just kidding!

Read Song of Songs 1:1–11. "We will make you earrings of gold, studded with silver." Impractical.

I hate to admit this, but I feel like I need to share what I did once so you'll know that I can relate. The first Christmas that Lisa and I were married, I blew it major-league in the impracticality department. It was 4:45 p.m. on Christmas Eve and the stores in Houston were closing in fifteen minutes. I was hanging out with my best friend and decided to rush into the first department store we saw. I told the clerk, "Yeah, I'll take that bathrobe. Size small (I forgot that Lisa is almost 5'9"). Yeah, that's great, whatever. Here's your twenty-five bucks."

I honestly thought that it was a great gift for Lisa. It was something she could use. Practical. To make it worse, I didn't even bother to wrap it. Well, needless to say that when I handed it to her, she was not a happy camper. It wasn't so much that I gave her a bathrobe. The problem was that I didn't think about it, I didn't plan for it, and I definitely didn't stretch myself and use my creativity in making the purchase.

The final thing for you to do as a husband is *give compliments.* Women need compliments, especially public acknowledgments. In fact, they thrive on them. If you even say an off-the-cuff, negative kind of thing to your wife, it can destroy her self-esteem. But if you say something genuinely complimentary, she'll feel like a queen, your queen. Your wife, as do all wives, looks to you as her husband for value and affirmation. Compliment her privately, too. Stay away from being critical and trying to control your wife by trying to make her into a woman she is not.

A good friend of mine, Pastor Jentezen Franklin, confessed in a sermon that trying to change his wife was one of the biggest mistakes he made early in his marriage. He wanted her to "act like a preacher's wife," instead of allowing her time and space to evolve using her God-given gifts. It was a constant source of struggle in their marriage until he learned to appreciate her for who she is.

Compliments are important to women and, therefore, important to the quality and stability of the marriage. Solomon wrote poetry to his bride that was full of compliments.

"You're so beautiful, my darling, so beautiful, and your dove eyes are veiled by your hair as it flows and shimmers, like a flock of goats in the distance streaming down a hillside in the sunshine. Your smile is generous and full—expressive and strong and clean. Your lips are jewel red, your mouth elegant and inviting, your veiled cheeks soft and radiant. The smooth, lithe lines of your neck command notice— all heads turn in awe and admiration! Your breasts are like fawns, twins of a gazelle, grazing among the first spring flowers."*

Notice he was specific. Be specific in your compliments to your wife. Don't just say, "Well yeah, that was a pretty good meal, baby." Say something specific like "I really like the way you put the cut-up fruit all around the edges. All the dishes really came together well. It was unbelievable. It really was."

I can't even begin to explain the meanings behind many of the words in the Song of Songs. It's really very interesting stuff, so please take the time to read it and research it. Invest in a good commentary to help you understand it better, and buy a Bible that uses contemporary language and read it.

Solomon used the language and tools of his day to keep his marriage strong. Today we would say he had game! He laid some very, very vivid and direct stuff on his wife, and it worked, because they were very intimate with each other.

A Succesexful Wife (from Lisa)

Men think about sex more than women do. That's been proven in study after study. Men think about sex more than twice as often as women.† That's probably no real surprise, as a wife, is it? What may

---

* *The Message* paraphrase.
† *Sexual Intimacy in Marriage* by William Cutrer and Sandra Glahn (Grand Rapids, MI: Kregel Publications), p. 87.

be a surprise, though, is that husbands want their wives to be more aggressive sexually. Solomon's wife was sexually aggressive.

It's so important for women to know you can *be more aggressive sexually*. The Sexperiment is a good time to practice how to be more aggressive. Now, I realize that suggestion may ruffle some ladylike feathers. Maybe you were brought up to believe that nice girls aren't supposed to want sex, so you suppress the urge to initiate sex with your husband. But he needs to know that you desire him. Yes, your husband is used to being the aggressor, but it makes him feel good when you let him know that *you* want *him* in bed.

Most young wives don't understand their husbands' mentality about sex. Early on, I had a difficult time understanding what a man's sex drive is like. But because I asked Ed questions and listened to the answers, I began to see how my husband looks at sex, how he thinks about sex, and how I can approach him in ways that communicate my love and desire for him.

In Song of Songs 7:1, Solomon and his wife are alone in the palace. She put on a sheer negligee, stepped into a pair of sexy sandals, and she did a dance of the Mahanaim for her man. Now, we don't know what the dance of the Mahanaim was, but the Shulamite knew it would arouse her husband. She was a wise wife because she knew that men are aroused more by sight, and she approached him visually.

Spouses tend to approach each other the way they want to be approached, but that's not the most effective way to get close to your mate. Wives, step outside of yourself and what you want in order to see what your husband wants.

The Sexperiment is a good time to start getting to know what pleases your husband. Don't just assume that as long as he's getting sex he'll be happy. The Shulamite knew her husband well enough to know what would arouse him. And here is how Solomon responded to her: "How beautiful are your feet in sandals, O prince's daughter! The curves of your thighs are like jewels, the work of the hands of a skillful workman."*

---

* Song of Solomon 7:1, NKJV

Wouldn't you love to hear your husband say those kinds of words to you? What are you willing to give up in order to hear him talk to you that way?

Be more aggressive. Take the initiative. And if you're feeling unsure, pray about it: "God, my husband has a stronger sex drive than I do. Help me to have a sex drive that is more complementary to his. Help me to understand his sexual drive so that I can meet him where he needs to be met."

You see, sex is not some selfish thing you do (or don't do) when you feel like it. As you engage in the Sexperiment with your husband, I encourage you to slow down to fully benefit from your week of intentional sexual intimacy. If you invest more of yourself into the Sexperiment, you'll get more in return.

The world says, "Get what you can while you can." God says, "Focus on giving, and the getting will take care of itself. The husband gives himself to the wife. The wife gives herself to the husband."

The second thing wives can learn from the Shulamite woman is, *make yourself available*. She was available. She wasn't telling her husband, "Not tonight, I have a headache." She was living what the apostle Paul expressed in 1 Corinthians 7:4–5: "The wife's body does not belong to her alone but also to her husband. In the same way, the husband's body does not belong to him alone but also to his wife."

The Bible tells married couples, "Do not deprive each other except by mutual consent and for a time that you may devote yourselves to prayer." Wives, this does not mean that you change your excuse from "No, I have a headache" to "No, I am in prayer." Temporary abstinence in marriage has to be a mutual decision.

When you say no regularly to your spouse, you are in danger of having your fellowship broken. Not your relationship, not your salvation, but your fellowship. When you keep on saying "no, no, no" to your husband, it hurts his self-esteem. It can also tempt him, or you, into adultery.

The Sexperiment will be your week of saying "yes," and in so doing you can begin to see the benefit. You will say yes to sex. Yes to fulfillment. Yes to greater and deeper intimacy. Yes to engaging as a couple on another level.

God gives us many more yeses than noes. The noes are reserved for those things that will hurt our fellowship with Him. The yeses are to bring intimacy into our relationship with Him. Saying yes to your spouse brings intimacy and growth.

Have you ever gone on a diet before? If you have, then you know that while you're on the diet, all you think about is food. When one spouse is forced to be on a sexual diet because the other spouse says "no, no, no" all the time, it causes the denied spouse to concentrate on sex even more.

When no is unavoidable, like when one of you, or the kids, is really tired or sick or whatever, you can work things out and say, "OK, I'm going to say no tonight, but I'll give you a specific time tomorrow when we can come together in marriage." It's so important to do this, because there are so many temptations out there. We live in a sex-crazed culture and we must make ourselves available to our spouse.

Third, wives, *use your imagination*. Don't put your imagination away in the drawer before you and your husband make love. The Shulamite told her husband, "...at our door is every delicacy, both new and old, that I have stored up for you, my lover."* Then she goes on enticing him, telling him they will make love outdoors.

Wives, you have a choice: you can be a sexual Rembrandt or you can remain a paint-by-numbers sex partner. God wants you to progress, along with your husband, to the Rembrandt stage. He wants you to use all of your divinely inspired creativity in the bedroom with your spouse. You wouldn't think of serving your husband the same frozen TV dinner every night. Use your creativity to ensure you're not serving your husband the same frozen sexual response night after night after night. Think sexy thoughts and think like your husband. Planning a party, you think about the details to make the party festive. You go to extra lengths to establish a mood and

---

* Song of Songs 7:13

environment. Give sex with your spouse that same kind of attention to detail and imagination.

Finally, wives, *speak candidly*. The Shulamite woman shared her positive feelings with her husband. "How handsome you are, my lover! Oh, how charming!"* Ed already shared with the husbands that wives like compliments. Well, men like them, too. They like to hear us say good things about them. Our words give feelings of worth and accomplishment to our husbands.

One of the rules of healthy marriage is that wives (and husbands, too) need to be able to speak candidly to each other. I'm not talking about brutal honesty that is insensitive, unkind, or hurtful. But achieving fulfillment in marriage requires honesty.

Before you begin your Sexperiment, I encourage you to go with your husband to a quiet restaurant or some other neutral space, get away from everything, and talk specifically about what pleases you in this beautiful gift from God called sex. Through your open and honest communication, hopefully and prayerfully the walls that have divided you and your spouse will come down. This will be a great time for you to start the process toward understanding each other, knowing what it takes to meet the other's needs and really understanding what God's word means when it talks about having a great sex life.

To help you begin your dialogue, here are a few tips about sexuality that most people miss.

1. Set goals. To intentionally get somewhere, you must first know where you're heading. Sit down with your spouse and set goals about what you want to learn about one another sexually. Talk about how often you hope to have sex and other tangible areas that relate to your sex life with each other.

2. Learn to explore. You don't know as much about your spouse's body as you think you do. Ask questions about what brings pleasure to your spouse.

---

* Song of Songs 1:16

3. *You are not a mind reader.* Hopefully, as you grow old together, you will come to know your spouse deeply and truly intimately. But no matter how close your bond, you will never master the thought processes of your husband. Therefore, communicate. Ask questions and be willing to receive answers.

4. *Your spouse is not a mind reader.* Don't keep your feelings in a fragile bowl, thinking, "If he really cared, he would know how I feel." Share your feelings, desires, and even concerns in an appealing and appropriate manner.

Get in There and Do It!

The Sexperiment is not a gimmick. It's real and it involves a lot more than just having sex for seven days. This first chapter has presented a lot of information for husbands and wives to absorb, and requires serious effort to negotiate some difficult stuff.

For some, the challenge week will reignite the fires of passion. You'll get back to a place in your relationship that you have longed to return to, but for whatever reasons haven't been able to reach.

Even so, I know that some of you have wounds so deep that you're not particularly excited about a week of sex. While some couples will eagerly anticipate a week of sex, challenging though it may be, seven days of sex will cause some repressed or negative feelings to rise to the surface for many other couples. Perhaps betrayal, unavailability, criticism, rejection, or infidelity has torn away at the fibers of your marital bond and your marriage is threadbare.

"She's said no so many times, I'm tired of being turned down, so I just quit trying."

Rejection is painful, especially when it happens continuously. You need to tell your wife how you feel about her rejection. Sometimes women think that rejection doesn't affect men, as if we have a polyurethane coating over our feelings. She needs to hear from you that it's not true.

"Lisa, I just can't forget what he did. I don't trust him anymore. He says he's sorry and it won't happen again, but how can I believe him?"

Betrayal is a major hurdle to overcome and it takes time. But at the same time, your marriage can't move forward if you're stuck in a pit of unforgiveness. Let him know how you feel and how badly you were hurt by his betrayal. Then take a giant step toward forgiveness. Give him a chance to earn your trust again.

During the Sexperiment, whether your marriage bond is strong or frayed, you'll be forced to talk about issues and confront problems that may have been buried for a long time. It may even drive you to the doorstep of a counselor. Don't shy away from that. Meet it head-on.

Guys, in particular, are often hesitant to pick up the phone to call a Christian counselor. But if you're willing to hire a swing coach for your golf game, a trainer for your workout, or a mechanic for your car, you should be more than willing to hire a "coach" to help you in the most important earthly relationship you will ever be a part of.

This challenge is about strengthening your marriage, so if it takes counseling to get to that place of strength, then do it!

Whatever the Sexperiment produces in your marriage, I want to encourage you to not make this a legalistic venture. It's purposeful, but fun. Don't get caught up in details like, "Well, I'm traveling from Wednesday to Friday, so what should we do?" or "I have a sick child at home who needs more attention," or "An unexpected deadline at work just popped up."

If you get caught up in the minutiae of the whens, hows, and wheres, you'll miss the bigger picture of *why*. Focus instead on doing what you can for your spouse, dealing with any issues that arise and connecting with the one whom God has given you.

Most of the time, when we talk about sex, we tend to blush and chuckle, but I really hope that you will dedicate yourselves to taking every aspect of the Sexperiment seriously. It does work! There are few things that bring so much benefit while at the same time giving so much pleasure.

Lisa and I hope that the Sexperiment will set you and your spouse on the path to a solid foundation of marital fulfillment. We have a God-given gift—sex—and we're to use this God-given gift in a life-uniting covenant called marriage.

As you will find out, your challenge week will force you to bring your best game to the marital equation. And as you do, you'll re-ignite some of those marital fires, open up the lines of communication, and find yourself on the right trajectory to help you and your spouse get the most out of your life together. Your experience can be just like this one:

> Wow, what an impact [the Sexperiment] has made in our lives! My marriage has been festering with pain and anguish over past betrayal, deep wounds from scathing words spoken, and a general sense of brokenness. Out of obedience to God, I decided to partici-pate in [the Sexperiment] and I'm so thankful I did. I've prayed for healing for our marriage for years, but it wasn't until I made the decision to do this out of service and love for my husband and God that I have begun to feel some restoration in our relationship.

So if you're ready to discover all of that and so much more, begin the challenge. Now get in there and start having sex!

Action Steps

1. Sit down with your spouse to plan a time to begin your Sex-periment, keeping in mind that there will never be a perfect time.

2. Make preparations before you begin so you can eliminate as many barriers to intimacy as possible (for example, hiring babysitters, making dinner reservations, rescheduling appointments, etc.).

3. Discuss the outcome you're hoping for after completing your first Sexperiment.

4. Take the necessary measures to clear up any lingering friction between you before the Sexperiment begins, or at least agree that past issues will not be allowed to interfere.

5. Pray together and separately before your Sexperiment begins. Ask God to grant a right spirit in you that is more interested in giving to and pleasing your spouse than in receiving.

—————— *Before You Do* ——————

*Y*ou may have read this first chapter and decided, "That will never happen to us. We'll never get tired of each other because we won't allow anything to come between us as husband and wife." That's a good goal to have, but the reality of marriage, and the experiences of thousands of married couples, says it can, and probably will happen in your marriage. The good news is, when you know it's a possibility, you can be on your guard against intimacy killers.

Before you cross the threshold, talk seriously about your expectations, including sex. As an engaged couple, you have the opportunity to establish open and honest communication with each other now. If you're not in premarital counseling, please sign up for it. Your counselor can even guide you through conversations about what you should expect from each other sexually . . . not details, but a general understanding of expectations about sex. Know how often your future spouse wants to have sex. Discuss "off-limits" behavior and sexual "turnoffs." Some issues can only be resolved within the context of matrimony; however, your period of engagement is not too early to lay the foundation for marital intimacy through honesty and communication.

The best counseling will be with a counselor who approaches everything from a biblical standpoint. When a counselor who is trained and educated with what it takes to guide couples combines that training with knowledge and direction from the Bible, you are well on your way to success as a couple.

──────── *The Yoke Is Not a Joke* ────────

*I*t's impossible to work on marital issues without being married. But don't get into such a hurry that you marry a person who's not a good match for you. Take seriously the Bible's advice to be equally yoked (joined). It may lower the frequency of your dating, but it will definitely increase the quality of your dating.

God's word cautions us against being joined with the wrong person.* It is so important to be properly united in marriage, and as a single person, you have the opportunity to ensure that, going forward, you date only potential partners with whom you are equally aligned.

While you wait for the right mate, what you can do is work on bringing your best self to your future marriage relationship. If you've been married before and hope to remarry, think about barriers to intimacy that arose in your previous marriage. And if you haven't been in counseling, consider it to ensure that you don't bring old relationship issues into a future relationship.

Since you're not going to have sex for seven days, try doing something else that constitutes worship that serves someone else. After all, marriage is about giving. You can volunteer to read at a homeless shelter for women and children or perform some type of service for seven elderly people.

───────

* 2 Corinthians 6:14

Perhaps you realize that your relationship with God isn't what it should be. This relationship should be your number-one concern. Focus this week on building intimacy with God. Begin by spending time each day alone with God in prayer. Tell Him how much you love and adore Him. Thank Him for the ways He has moved in your life. In your time with God, you can use your creativity in coming to God and make yourself fully available to Him. And as you offer your love and appreciation to God, hear Him as He tells you that He loves you, that you are important to Him and how much He wants you to have the best in your life.

2

Stop Making Sexcuses...
and Start Making Love

A few years ago, Lisa and I went to my thirtieth high school reunion. It was amazing to see so many people from the past and to catch up with what is happening in their lives, where they've gone and what they've done. But there's something interesting about reunions. It's a time when we try to bring "back then" into "right now." The venue was rocking and the décor matched the look, feel, and vibe of the year we graduated—it was definitely very seventies. The reunion committee really did a great job of reaching back into the past and bringing it to the present. They were keeping the past current.

After the reunion I thought a bit more about that concept of keeping the past current. It made me think about marriage, because a great marriage does the same thing. We take the past and bring it into the present. We take the past—the vows we took, the thoughtfulness we employed, and the passion we felt—and try to keep it relevant, day to day.

But that happens by design, not by accident. We make an intentional effort to keep our vows current. We put forth an intentional effort to keep our commitment to the marriage current. Husbands and wives have to put forth an intentional effort to keep a relationship fresh and alive and engaging. Your decision to take on the Sexperiment is a great step toward that kind of intentionality. It could be the first step in restoring the vibrancy of true intimacy to your marriage.

People try to recapture their youth during class reunion time. They go to great lengths to rekindle friendships, and maybe even old romances for the single people. That's what should be happening in marriage. Of course, people grow in marriage, and they should. Lisa and I are not the same people we were when we married back in the 1980s. No couple should strive to stay exactly as they were when they got married. What they should strive to maintain or recapture, however, is the romance, consideration, and intimacy they shared early in marriage.

In all the years—decades, really—that I've been a pastor, I've officiated more weddings than I can count. I know all sorts of vows. And when a bride and a groom recite the vows, most of them are totally on another planet. It's like they're having an out-of-body experience. I know that was true for Lisa and me. Couples don't fully grasp what they're saying. And they certainly don't understand all the implications of those vows. It takes a while before the reality of those vows set in. A great marriage, though, is going to keep those vows current long after you become fully aware of their meaning.

So as you take the Sexperiment, I want you to retrieve and revive your vows—even if you took them only six months ago. Recite those vows to your spouse before beginning the challenge, and then do it regularly, perhaps once a month.

"But you don't understand. It's been a long time since we recited our vows. I don't even remember what we said!"

There are some great biblical wedding vows online to choose from to recite to each other. Repeating your vows regularly helps couples to remember the bond they share, something sacred between them and God.

The notion of a continuous renewal of the marital bond sounds great, and it is. It's common knowledge, even to the point of becoming cliché, that married couples want closeness and sexual intimacy, but often don't have it as much as they'd like. For many, the responsibilities of family and work overwhelm their best efforts at intimacy. Many of you have picked up this book and committed to the Sexperiment because you want to get back to a place of physical, emotional, psychological, and spiritual closeness in marriage.

Having the desire for closeness and intimacy is not enough, though. Many couples long for closeness, but somehow life gets in the way. Unresolved issues and real-life responsibilities can interrupt the flow of intimacy in marriage. Their closeness meter gets thrown off center point and gets out of balance.

Feng shui (pronounced fung SHWAY) is an ancient Chinese practice that was used thousands of years before the invention of the compass as a measuring system to bring harmony and balance into architecture and life. In more modern usages, architects, decorators, and professional organizers are adopting this concept to help people bring harmony into their homes and workspaces. Any of them will tell you that clutter is a major obstacle to achieving feng shui.

A lot of marriages could use a little feng shui. When the "vibe" is off in your marriage, it usually leads to the absence of sex. And just like with your physical environment, clutter can be a major barrier to intimacy in marriage. I'm not talking about physical clutter right now (though decorators and organizers will tell you that's a major romance killer too). Intimacy in marriage can be blocked by too much mental and emotional clutter—I call them "sexcuses."

Maybe you think your marriage is unique, but every couple deals with similar sexcuses that block intimacy—work, kids, unresolved feelings, lack of time and lack of motivation—no marriage is immune. The enemy wants husbands and wives to fall into a pit of boredom and routine because he wants us to regard marriage as misery. He wants us to divorce, to have extramarital affairs, to be consumed with Internet porn, and to spend precious time engaged in lustful thoughts instead of focusing on how to better serve our spouse.

Satan lures us into believing that our sexcuses are legitimate reasons not to be intimate. The spouse giving the sexcuses may feel they are totally valid, but they're really only a tool the enemy uses to drive a wedge between the husband and wife. That wedge doesn't have to be very wide to offer just enough wiggle room for someone or something else to come in and create a chasm and chaos.

Jesus affirmed that in marriage the two spouses become one: "Since they are no longer two but one, let no one split apart what God has joined together."* Maybe on your wedding day you were too nervous to think about much that the preacher said. If you had a Christian wedding service, you were warned on the first day of your marriage not to let anything create division in your covenant—not in-laws, not kids, not careers, not sexcuses. Then, after all the words and the vows, you and your spouse retreated down the aisle feeling like you were one: "It's us against the world."

Now, let's get back to the real world for a moment. After the initial glow of wedded bliss—be it days, weeks, months, or even years— at some point, life does get in the way of marital intimacy. One of the kids gets really sick. You have to work overtime until a major project is completed. A water pipe bursts and causes damage to the house. These things happen in life, but that's different from sexcuses that clutter up the relationship. Sexcuses are mental and emotional baggage that block intimacy and make it difficult for couples to stay bonded in marriage.

"But, honey, I'm tired!"

"I have a headache."

"There's not a free second in the calendar."

"I'm still mad about…"

"Do I look fat?"

"Kids. Kids. Kids."

"I'm just not in the mood."

Of course, bigger issues can get in the way, but for right now, we just need to deal with the little foxes that the Bible says ruin the vineyards.†

---

* Matthew 19:6, NLT

† Song of Songs 2:15

In the first chapter, we looked at the wisdom of Solomon and his bride in their marriage. But look at a paraphrase of the Bible and see what the Shulamite says in chapter two about the little foxes.

Solomon had asked her to come to him. She replied, "Then you must protect me from the foxes, foxes on the prowl. Foxes who would like nothing better than to get into our flowering garden."

She's saying that couples have to keep stuff from getting in the way of their special love relationship.

It's the responsibility of the husband and the wife to keep the little foxes, the clutter, away so there will be time, opportunity, and desire for making love.

Usually, the lack of sexual intimacy is not a mutual decision, but evolves out of too many sexcuses, and they don't always come from the woman.

Part of the problem is that sex becomes entangled in other issues and then it's used as a bargaining chip. Spouses should never use sex as a reward or as a weapon. *Never.* If you are hearing a constant refrain of "No, no, no," in the bedroom, whoever is saying no is wrong. Depriving a spouse of sexual intimacy is sin. The Bible tells husbands and wives, "Do not deprive each other except perhaps by mutual consent."*

Lisa and I have five dogs, and three of them weigh more than 100 pounds. They are monstrous, strong dogs and a bit scary at times. Since a typical fence cannot restrain them, we installed an underground electrical fence in our yard and the dogs wear special collars. When they get near the fence, it warns them with a beep and if they step over the line, it will shock them just enough to deter them from crossing the line.

When it comes to sex, some spouses can feel like they have a shock collar on. He tries to initiate: "Come on, baby. Tonight is the night." *Zzzzap!* He gets a shock: "Don't cross that boundary!"

At our house, we can turn the electric fence off and the dogs

---

* 1 Corinthians 7:5

don't even know it. They don't even bother to go near the fence any-more. A lot of spouses won't even bother to go near the intimacy zone anymore because they don't want to get zapped again.

When you react negatively to your spouse's advances, you can shame your spouse by your response. By constantly turning your spouse down, you are communicating that something must be wrong with his or her desires or that his or her needs are not legiti-mate. It takes a certain amount of vulnerability to ask for your sexual needs to be met, so it is embarrassing and defeating to be rejected.

In addition, negative responses can interfere with your fellow-ship with God. The sin of depriving your spouse of his or her sexual needs puts a strain on your fellowship with the Lord. The marriage relationship is a reflection of the relationship that Christ has with the church. Because of this unique correlation, when your marriage rela-tionship is strained, your relationship with Christ is also negatively affected.

Furthermore, through constant rejection you are inviting height-ened temptations for both you and your spouse. Sadly, when spouses do not get what they need at home, they often will go looking else-where for it.

Sometimes the demands of life really do get in the way of inti-macy. That's just life. There have been many times when Lisa and I have had to say no because of things that come up. But our "no" doesn't translate as personal rejection. No one should ever feel forced to have sex, even with a spouse. It's OK to say no, but say it with a caveat: "No. But how about tomorrow?" If you are feeding your spouse a constant diet of "no," then you are killing intimacy and sin-ning before God.

I know some husbands are cheering as they read this. OK, I hear that. But here's the other side of the coin. Some men treat their wives so poorly, what else should they expect? No wonder she's giving you sexcuses instead of sex.

One night, Lisa and I had dinner with a few people, and one of the couples present was a celebrity and his wife. During dinner, the conversation was flowing along and this man was telling us about some of his experiences. As he was telling us about his career and all that he had accomplished, he wrapped it up by saying, "My career is my first love. Nothing in the world is more important to me." The moment he said that we looked at his wife, and her countenance and demeanor reflected some serious feelings of rejection and hurt. As we watched his wife hang her head, we all sympathized with her in embarrassment and it was clear the intimacy and affection that were lacking. What more could be said?

Husbands, as leaders of the home, need to lead in the area of establishing the kind of environment that promotes intimacy. Leadership in the Bible—and that includes leadership in the home—begins with servanthood and ends with sacrifice. Some Christians make a big deal out of the Bible verse that says "Wives, submit to your husbands as to the Lord," and it is a big deal.* It's always a hot-button topic, guaranteed to stimulate discussion and all sorts of opinions. But there are a couple of caveats in this passage that rarely get addressed.

First is the servanthood issue, which is found just before that, in Ephesians 5:21: "Submit *to one another* out of reverence for Christ." It's amazing how that part gets glossed over. Husbands and wives are to submit to one another. Mutual submission means you're more concerned with meeting each other's needs than with fighting about who's in charge of the relationship.

Then comes the sacrifice part, which is found in Ephesians 5:25: "Husbands, love your wives, just as Christ loved the church and gave himself up for her . . ." I'm thoroughly convinced that if you love your wife enough to die for her, and demonstrate that depth of sacrifice in your marriage, she will have no trouble submitting to you and showing her gratitude for you by being loving and intimate in the relationship.

Husbands, you start serving and sacrificing, and just watch and see what happens. You might be amazed to find yourself married to

---

* Ephesians 5:22

a totally different woman. And here's where a lot of husbands mess up with this. As the leader of your home, your service and sacrifice should be demonstrated in ways that are important to her, not in the ways you *think* should be important to her.

Marriage should be a serving contest between a husband and wife. Constantly look for opportunities to consider your spouse's needs. As you take the Sexperiment, you will be reminded of what it means to serve each other.

Successful completion of the challenge requires both spouses to put service before self. That includes sexcuses. Let's look at a breakdown of the common marital sexcuses for what they really are.

"Not tonight, honey. I'm too tired."

It's no secret that the sex drive between a man and a woman is different, and it's also no secret that men and women have a difficult time understanding the difference in the way that their spouse thinks about sex.

In his book *Give & Take: The Secret to Marital Compatibility,* Christian psychologist Dr. Willard F. Harley Jr. has a wonderful illustration that really hammers home for the women an understanding of a man's sex drive and what a man goes through when he is rejected. Imagine a stool with a glass of water sitting on it. The husband is next to the stool and the wife is next to him. The wife, for some reason, is immobilized. Her husband is the only one who can get the water for her.

Here is what happens, Harley says. The wife turns to her husband: "Honey, would you please pour me a glass of water? I am getting thirsty."

The husband turns and responds, "I don't really feel like it right now. I am not in the mood; I'm a little tired; maybe in a couple of hours."

Hours roll by. One more time the wife turns to her husband: "Honey, I am getting thirsty. Would you please give me a glass of water?"

The husband responds, "Look, I told you I'm tired. I've had a long day, OK?"

Then the wife begins to get angry. She can feel her temperature rising. She wants a glass of water badly at this point, so she begins to demand a drink of water. "I want a glass of water. You are the only one who can give me the glass of water. Give me some water!"

The husband looks at his wife, spins on his heels, and says, "Well, you are not going to get any water with an attitude like that."

The husband returns to the scene about a day later and now the wife is livid. Finally, the husband says, "OK! Here is your water. Just drink it!"

When the wife is gulping down the water, do you think she is satisfied? Do you think her thirst is really quenched? Not really. She is thinking that she is going to be thirsty again, and if she wants another drink of water, she had better watch what she says to her husband.

So goes the human sex drive. Like water quenches a physical thirst, sex in marriage quenches each spouse's thirst in a physical, spiritual, emotional, and psychological manner. Sex must be given and received with a right spirit if it is to truly satisfy those longings.

"There's not a free second on the calendar."

Men are so compartmentalized, so structured, that most of us are brainless concerning the overall context of sex in the marital relationship. We are, for the most part, one-dimensional people. While boarding an airplane one time, I walked by a group of women. One of them was reading a book entitled, *All About Men*. So, I looked at her and said, "All about men, huh?"

She said, "Yeah, it's a short book."

I nearly died laughing.

The house could be dirty. You could have just been in a major argument five minutes earlier. If you are a man, you are still likely to pat your wife on her rear and say, "Hey, hey, hey. How about you and me head to the bedroom?"

Wives, on the other hand, are multifaceted and multidimensional. The context surrounding the sexual part of the relationship is huge for women. Wives have to know that everything is A-OK outside the master bedroom before everything gets A-OK between the sheets.

So what do we do about it? Yes, there are those times when the husband and wife are both in the mood, when they both want to make love. But what do you do when one is ready for it and the other is not (which is more often the case)?

Get into the pace of passion. Husbands, slow down. Quit being a sprinter all the time and go on a long-distance run with your wife. It's sometimes fun to jog. Wives, don't always run so slowly. Try incorporating some sprints into that 5K run.

When the husband is thinking about his wife's needs and the wife is thinking about her husband's needs, you have two people understanding the pace of passion. If you want to get your partner in the mood, approach him or her the way he or she wants and needs to be approached to elicit the response you desire.

"I have a headache."

No one has a headache all the time, even if you're prone to migraines. But if a wife, for example, always has a headache when her husband initiates sex, it's time to ask why and get to the root cause. After many men get married, they think, "Hey, I've got my spouse. I can lose the look and start working on my love handles. I can go on a hygiene hiatus, man. So what if I go play softball after work and come home and want a little lovin' before I take a shower? But she keeps telling me no."

Some men think that their look from ten, twenty, or thirty years ago is still good enough to attract their wife. The problem is that they are still walking around with that high school jock look, complete with the same old gym shorts, the tattered tank top, the rough and unshaven face, but with maybe more weight and less hair. He's thinking, "Hey, baby! In case you don't know, I've still got it!" Meanwhile, the wife is wondering how he could be so clueless as to why she doesn't want him to touch her.

In response to their hygienically challenged mates, wives don one of those "Not tonight, honey" nightgowns before bed. You know, the kind that screams, "I have a headache!"

We may laugh at these scenarios, but they represent a real-life problem in many marriages. After we say "I do," we often follow it up with "I don't" behavior. We put sex way down on the priority list of our marriage, so we don't try to maintain the body God has given to us.

"I'm still mad about..."

The Bible advises us not to let the sun go down on our anger.* That's a good guideline for human behavior, but especially for intimate relationships. I know that sometimes there are hurts in a relationship that we as human beings simply can't get over in a day. Infidelity, abusive behavior, meanness, and similar behaviors take time to get over and then to rebuild trust, usually with the help of a qualified Christian counselor.

But marriage can mean coping with a lot of little things that are blown up into bigger things because we won't forgive and let it go. That's usually something we can control. When we stay angry for days over fairly insignificant things, it's because we choose to allow them to fester and become more painful. Like, when he uses one of the decorative towels in the bathroom to wipe the excess shaving cream off his face (every husband knows that's against the rules), or when he forgets to do those things that are really important to you.

Husbands get mad, too, but when it comes to having sex we're much better at getting over whatever we were upset about. Rarely does a man let his upset get in the way of having sex! "So you gave my high school jersey to Goodwill? Never mind that it doesn't fit anymore. I was wearing it when we beat Westside High and won the

---

* Ephesians 4:26

state championship!" While he's still pitching a fit, she comes out of the bathroom wearing the negligee you bought her last Valentine's Day. You miss your jersey, but you're definitely not going to miss this opportunity to have sex.

When we allow anger to fester and grow, we give the devil a foothold in our relationship.* Have you ever thought about how much energy it takes to stay angry? You have to constantly relive the deed in your mind and summon enough emotion to stay angry about it. Whether it's a trifling matter or a major transgression that damages the relationship, at some point you have to let it go so you can move forward. And in the letting go, you will find your way back to harmony within yourself and, therefore, within your marriage.

In the Bible, Paul warns us to put aside our carnal nature. When most Christians hear the word *carnal*, they immediately think of sex, but our carnality includes so much more. Like anger. The word Paul uses for anger means yelling, volume.† Sometimes we get really angry when we get into arguments, but we do have the capacity to control ourselves and our responses.

I remember a particular time when Lisa and I were having a pretty intense argument. I was kind of raising my voice a little bit and the phone rang. Instantly, I was transformed from an angry person into a caring, compassionate pastor. "Hello? Oh, everything is great here. How are you doing? Thank you so much for calling. Oh, really? Oh, that's wonderful! Congratulations. When is it due? We will be praying for you. Thank you very much. Good-bye." And then I went right back into the argument. I had no problem extending courteous and mannered speech to my acquaintance on the phone. I should have made an even greater effort to extend courtesy to my wife, but I didn't. I blew it.

Another thing Paul mentions in that Bible passage is "hateful things." You know what the words *hateful things* mean in the original

---

* Ephesians 4:27
† Colossians 13:8

Greek language? It means pushing your spouse's hot button. When you have been married for a while, you know that little gesture, that little word, that little look that will send your spouse over the edge. When we get down and dirty in an argument, and we realize that it's mostly our fault, what do we do? We reach for that hot button and push. Let's get ready to rumble!

Lisa and I have a list of ground rules for couples about handling conflict, and we'll discuss those in another chapter. But one of those rules is: *Don't become a scorekeeper in your marriage.* Scorekeepers in marriage keep track of who's winning and who's losing. And usually the scorekeeper is determined not to lose. Newsflash: If you're playing scorekeeper in marriage, you both lose. Don't, don't, don't do the scorekeeper thing.

Another rule is: *Don't play the historian.* You know who the historian is, don't you? The historian looks back into your marital filing cabinet and brings back arguments and conflicts that were going on even in your dating relationship. Don't do that.

One time Lisa and I were in a conflict, and I must admit that my selfishness got the better of me. I was so focused on winning the argument that I brought up some issues from our high school dating days. Yes, high school!

Women have better memories than men and can recall all the details of past battles with amazing accuracy. Let those issues that have been dealt with and forgiven remain a part of history. Don't resurrect something that should stay buried.

Mature Christian love and forgiveness compel us to stick to the present and gently deal with the issue at hand.

If there is something from the past that hasn't been properly dealt with and forgiven, then discuss it at a peaceful time and get it resolved. Don't bring it up in the heat of an argument and confuse the issue.

"Do I look fat?"

This is definitely a girl thing, because a guy can think he's a real stud even when he's got love handles down to his knees. You absolutely should look your best and you should strive to be healthy. But if you can't fit into your wedding gown anymore, you shouldn't assume you're no longer sexy in the eyes of your husband.

Yes, guys are visual, and that's what gets our attention first. But the bottom line is this: men find confidence in a woman sexy, so if you feel bad and insecure about your body, what's he supposed to think about it? If you don't like the way you look, work to change it. But as you're making changes, decide to feel good about yourself. Look in the mirror every day and tell yourself that you're stamped with God's label, the top designer in all of creation. Tell yourself good things—that you're beautiful, that you're looking better every day, and that you're beautiful from the inside out, where it really counts.

Plus, asking a man a question like, "Do I look fat?" is really a setup for him, because we're task oriented. We're problem solvers. So when a wife indicates to her husband that she's not happy with her size or her weight, the novice husbands are going to start giving advice on how to lose weight or tone up. He'll say stuff like, "Oh, babe, all you need to do is to tighten up your waist and your thighs a little." This unsuspecting husband is trying to help his wife, based on a question she's asked, but when he does, she's hurt.

The bottom line is, be the best you can be with all that God has given you. Encourage each other in this regard.

"Kids. Kids. Kids."

Many couples think that having kids won't change the dynamic of their relationship. That is wishful thinking and unrealistic at best!

Did you know that the word "kids" is really an acronym? It stands for *Keeping Intimacy at a Distance Successfully*. Having children requires some major structural changes in your life and your marriage. Where most couples get sidetracked, however, is making their marriage kid-centric instead of marriage-centric.

I wrote a book titled *Kid CEO* because in a number of households, the kids are running the show. The kids are in the corner office dictating how the parents live. They're calling the shots and putting a serious downer on the parents' lovemaking.

The lie of our culture is that the kids are the nucleus of the family cell. That is ludicrous, and it's not biblical. The *marriage* is the nucleus of the family cell. Lisa and I made the choice many years ago to make our family spouse-centric, and I'll tell you how it played out in our home when our kids were younger and we were teaching them about the importance of our marriage.

I usually arrive home by five thirty or six p.m. I walk in the door and greet the kids by giving them kisses and hugs. Then I usually proceed directly into the kitchen. Most of the time, Lisa and I will spend some time talking in the kitchen, so I'll turn and say something to the children like, "For the next twenty or thirty minutes, don't come into the kitchen. Your mother and I are going to talk. Now, if there's bloodshed, come in. Other than that, you just go and play."

Now that our kids are older (two are teenagers and two are in their twenties), they understand the priority we place on our marriage. And we began teaching them that from a very early age.

Parents, I challenge you to not let your kids control the romance meter in your marriage. Your children need to know that alone time is important to Mom and Dad. When you determine to make it a priority in your marriage, they will learn to accept it.

As parents, the best thing you can do for your children is to have a great marriage, because 24/7, your children are watching you. How else will they know about communication in relationships? How else will they know about appropriate levels of intimacy in relationships? How else will they know about forgiveness? How else will they know about love? About spiritual things?

Making love for the seven days of the Sexperiment will help parents realign their agenda with God's agenda. The challenge will help couples realize that in the order of the family, God comes first. Right behind that is the marriage. Then come the children. Having kids requires you to do a bit of extra planning to start the challenge.

My husband and I managed five days. It's difficult to make time for this kind of stuff with three children in the home, ages 11, 9 and 7. I'd say it was quite an accomplishment and we were very nice to one another.

It may not sound very romantic, but establishing a time for intimacy will help you complete the Sexperiment, but it also will help you establish the regular pattern of intimacy that your marriage needs. If you've allowed your children to sleep in your bed, the challenge will be a good time to begin teaching them that Mommy and Daddy's bed is for them only. Your bedroom should be a sanctuary for romance and rest. Your children have their own beds and should be sleeping in them. Additionally, your children should respect a closed door. Teach them to knock and respect privacy.

Give the kids a structured bedtime so that you can plan your time alone. Then, hire a sitter and go away for a night or two, every six months, even if it's just across town to the Motel 6. Go away for romance, go away for intimacy, and go away for sex. Taking these breaks is worth it and will reap huge benefits in your marriage. When you're away, the kids won't be a sexcuse that blocks intimacy.

"I'm just not in the mood."

If one spouse is never in the mood, something's wrong. The first thing should be to rule out any physiological, mental, or spiritual causes—medications that can affect libido, depression, or lingering unforgiveness. These issues should be handled with compassion and care. A lot of factors can affect libido in the human body. For example, a man may be reluctant to admit he has problems with erectile dysfunction, so he may simply tell his wife, "I'm just not in the mood."

But in dealing with the day-to-day issues of sexual desire, the reality is that rarely are both parties equally "in the mood." Usually one is more revved up than the other. This is a critical issue in marriage. A lot is hanging in the balance on this one. It's perfectly acceptable to say no, but no should be the exception, not the rule. It's the twenty-four-hour rule.

If "no" is regularly the reply to a spouse's advances, it will cause serious damage to his or her confidence, security, and ego. I truly believe that God holds us accountable regarding how we satisfy our mate sexually.

When you said "I do," you were committing to have sex with each other exclusively for the rest of your life. If you're reading this book and your spouse is lying next to you, then you're looking at your best and only sexual option! What a responsibility we have to enthusiastically satisfy our spouse's sexual desires!

It's essential to get to the root of any "not in the mood" issues. Sometimes it's because we've tiptoed around the boundaries that God set for marriage. Here's one husband's confession:

> I just want to get this out there, because it seems like I am the only husband who's at fault for not "wanting it" often enough. It seems that the husbands are always to blame for having affairs, and the women are to blame here for not "satisfying" their husband enough.
>
> I am the opposite. There haven't been any affairs in our marriage, thank God, but I don't seem to have the zest for being intimate with my wife like I should. I think what Ed has said about all the ways culture portrays sex might be part of my problem. Like he said, what culture says is a pipe dream. It's not reality. No one woman can satisfy all the images and fantasies that we see all over the place in our society. It's a problem in my mind, and like Ed said, problems out of the bed do affect problems into the bedroom . . .
>
> Please pray for my mind to wash all that out so that I can give my wife her seven days that she deserves, that I look forward to it like most husbands do.

Sexcuses Be Gone!

There's no way around it. We have a responsibility to satisfy our mate sexually. The Bible says we are to keep them so satisfied, in fact, that it takes away the flash and the dash and a lot of the power of the lure of lust. Lisa and I have applied this biblical mandate to our marriage, and great things have resulted from it.

The Bible says that the math of marriage is one plus one equals one. We are to look for this oneness. We are to have a common faith in Jesus Christ, we are to have community together, and then we are to express the act of sex in marriage.

Sex is like a Ferrari. If someone gives you a Ferrari, you don't trash it. You don't take it four-wheeling up the side of a steep hill. You take care of the Ferrari. You wash it and wax it. You put only the best fuel in it. You drive it on the Autobahn if you can. You drive it on the freeway. That is what a Ferrari is for.

So many, though, have this gift of sex, this Ferrari, and we haven't taken care of it. We haven't given it the proper maintenance. We've trashed it and we have abused it and made it almost worthless.

A Ferrari is a Ferrari, even when it's been abused or neglected. Once you start giving it proper care and maintaining it according to the owner's manual, it will return to giving the optimal performance it was designed to give.

You'll be amazed at what happens with this Ferrari (otherwise known as sex in marriage) when you do the Sexperiment. Your enhanced sex life with your spouse will cause you to seek God in a deeper way, in a more profound way, and even in a more passionate way. Sexual intercourse between a husband and a wife reflects the nature and character of God. The feminine aspects join with the masculine aspects of God. Intercourse is so beautiful, and when it is practiced by a husband and wife, it can be so worshipful that words cannot describe the experience.

It's not easy in today's culture, though, to have sex regularly because we're all speeding down Busy Boulevard. We have to slow down and be intentional about lovemaking and intimacy in marriage. We have to schedule it in and make it happen. No more sexcuses.

In marriage, as we fulfill each other sexually, it will free us up to hear from God in a deeper way. Abstinence in a marriage can distract you from hearing the voice of God. Abandon the sexcuses for the sake of your marriage and for the sake of your relationship with God. The spiritual and physical benefits are profound.

Action Steps

1. Make a list of the sexcuses that have blocked intimacy in your marriage. Discuss your feelings about them and make a firm commitment that none of them will be reasons for not completing the Sexperiment.

2. Make plans and preparations to overcome your sexcuses during the Sexperiment. Choose a week when you're less likely to be overwhelmed with work. Make sure the kids have enough clean clothes to get through the week. Prepare meals and freeze them for later in the week. Use your lunch break to take a nap at work so you won't be so tired when you get home. Set boundaries with your kids so they don't get in the way of your private time together. Do all that you can to demonstrate to each other that the Sexperiment will be a priority and an earnest endeavor to maintain or restore intimacy in your marriage.

3. If your marital intimacy is hindered by lots of sexcuses, make it a practice to look at the real issues behind them and deal with it. Ask yourself, "Am I making a sexcuse? What's really going on with me? With us? Why am I looking for a reason not to have sex?"

——— *Before You Do* ———

*C*onflict in any relationship is inevitable. Basically, all conflict can be summed up in three letters. I think almost all conflict centers on PMS. Now, before the ladies rip this book apart, let me explain.

P = Power. Who is going to call the final shot? Who is going to defer to whom?

M = Money. Is one of you a free spender and the other a saver? That could cause conflict.

S = Sex. What happens when one spouse is in the mood and the other spouse is not?

As a couple planning to marry, you have to talk about PMS and discuss how you plan to deal with it. Proverbs 15:22 says, "Plans fail for lack of counsel, but with many advisors they succeed." Many engaged couples think they don't need marital counseling. Whether this is your first time at the altar or even if you've had multiple marriages, don't let pride, ego, arrogance, or ignorance keep you from getting the wise counsel you need to establish a solid marriage.

Maybe you think, "Oh, we can just figure it out for ourselves. We're both smart people. We successfully manage conflict on the job all the time." It's not about what's in your head.

Author/psychologist M. Scott Peck observed in his book *The Road Less Traveled* that the sensation of falling in love is God's way of "tricking" us into marriage. That's an interesting way to look at it. But it's certainly true that when we're in love, we don't always enter into marriage with our eyes wide open and our brains turned on.

Before you marry, discuss your issues and expectations related to power, money, and sex to head off trouble down the road.

The Yoke Is Not a Joke

*D*oes the person you're dating seem to have any interest in pleasing you? You need to pay attention to that because that same spirit will transfer into a marriage with that person. Does he or she seem concerned about what's important to you? The restaurants you like? The social activities you like?

A critical component of marriage is the desire and willingness to serve and sacrifice. Someone who does not appear to want to please you in dating will not be concerned with meeting your needs in marriage.

The yoke is not a joke. Pay attention to the traits of the people you date. If you're the one making all of the concessions, if you're the only person sacrificing and serving for the sake of building or sustaining a relationship, it's time to bail and keep looking.

Women especially tend to fantasize that they can change a man or that, once the vows are made, he will magically become the loving, caring provider and leader of the home that she's always wanted. That's not always the case! People are who they are. If she's a self-absorbed girlfriend, she'll be a self-absorbed wife. If he's a cold and unfeeling boyfriend, he'll be a cold and unfeeling husband.

So many people walk into marriages that are doomed from the beginning because they fear no one else will come along or they convince themselves that since no one is perfect, they will learn to live with the other person's selfishness and lack of consideration. This was never a part of God's design for marriage. It's true that no one is perfect, but that should never be an excuse for accepting less than God's best for you in a mate.

3

The Math of Marriage

$\mathcal{L}$isa and I have been married for almost thirty years, and we have four children. I remember a particular family vacation when we got two hotel rooms, one for the children and one for us. One of our twin girls, said, "Hey, Mom, Dad. I know why you guys have your own room."

I replied, "Oh, really? Why is that, Landra?"

"So you guys can 'do your thing.'"

"That's right," I said. "That's why we got our own room, so we can 'do our thing.'"

It's good that our kids know that we "do our thing" and share intimacy as a married couple. They know that intimacy is important enough to us to make time and space for it. We block others out, and that sends an important message to our children that intimacy is something just for us as a husband and wife. And our kids understand that because, like I mentioned earlier, we've been teaching them that for years.

When you first think about it, you might think that the most inseparable human bond is the parent-child relationship, which is a blood connection. But that is not the case. For just a minute, forget the fact that I am a pastor writing this book. Practically speaking, let's look at the idea that marriage is the most important relationship. When your kids get older, what do you want to happen? You want them to move out! And when they do, who is left in the house? You and your spouse. So, it makes sense to work on your marriage, to strengthen your marriage now.

As a Christ follower, I place a much higher priority on God's Word than I do conventional wisdom. So I want to approach this idea from what God says. God says in His word that something powerful and magnetic will transpire when a man loves a woman and unites with her in a God-ordained relationship. The Bible tells us "man will leave his father and mother and be united to his wife, and they will become one flesh."*

When a man and a woman decide they want to spend their lives together, have children, and grow old with each other, they are choosing to realign the close blood bond with their parents as their primary relationship and join together in marriage. At that point, God tells us, a one-flesh relationship will evolve. In the Hebrew language, the term for "one flesh" means *to be melted together, to be inseparably linked.* What was once two completely separate parts has become one unified whole. You can't get the pieces apart.

Have you ever noticed that people who've been married a long time tend to look alike? That's oneness. When two people with totally different DNA spend enough time together and share enough experiences, their oneness transcends even to their physical appearance.

Oneness in marriage is two becoming one. That's the math of marriage—one plus one equals one. After the beautiful wedding ceremony and the solemn marriage vows, two people—fallen and fallible, self-centered and sinful—set out on a lifelong journey of becoming one. The key word here is *becoming.*

The Bible's charge and challenge issued to husbands and wives is "The two *shall become* one," not "The two *are* one." When I look at my wife, Lisa, I see reflected off of her Ed at his best and Ed at his worst. And she sees, in me, Lisa at her best and Lisa at her worst.

---

* Genesis 2:24

That's the way marriage is. And the longer you're together, the longer you walk in sync with each other, the more you see your best and the more you see your worst. But it is a process. Oneness in marriage is a process that requires sacrificial giving and loving service in mutual submission.

There are many dynamics that contribute to the becoming-one process, and sexual intimacy is a significant one, as you will discover during the Sexperiment. Many married couples occupy the same household for years without growing toward true oneness. Their relationships are fragmented and sexual intimacy is nonexistent. They may even be sleeping in separate bedrooms. Sadly they miss out on the fulfillment that comes from growing as one.

So, how do we become one? How do a man and a woman walk in unity? Ephesians 5:22 tells wives to submit to their husbands "as to the Lord." And Ephesians 5:25 tells husbands to love their wives, "as Christ loved the church." So, we have to get our "as" in gear! Getting our *as* in gear—as Christ, that is—gives us the ability and the octane to have an amazing marriage. When we adopt the marriage model of the Bible, everything is *as Christ*.

The number one is an integer; it's a whole number. The old band Three Dog Night sang, "One is the loneliest number that you'll ever do." But in marriage, one is the "onliest" number that you'll ever do. One in marriage is not loneliness; it is wholeness and holiness. When we're together in marriage, we have this wholeness thing going because God is into wholeness and holiness. So when we bolt on a marriage, either physically or emotionally, we become a fraction of what God wants us to be. And there are too many people who are living in fractions rather than in wholeness.

When I talk about bolting on marriage, I'm not referring only to divorce. When you have an extramarital affair, you bolt on your marriage and become a fraction of what God wants you to be. When you develop an intimate emotional attachment to someone other than your spouse, you bolt on your marriage and reduce yourself to a fraction of what God wants you to be. When sexual intimacy is lacking in your marriage, you, your spouse, and your marriage become a fraction of what God intends.

Sex is the God-given desire that brings the marital fire! Sex is the exclusive expression of the covenantal bond between a husband and wife. When you get married, your sex life with your spouse will cause you to seek God in a deeper way, in a more profound way, and even in a more passionate way.

Is sex really that big of a deal? I mean, beyond the physical pleasure and release that it brings?

Yes, it really is. Sexual intimacy in marriage is not a bunch of hype. It's real and it's essential to building oneness. Many couples need help getting to that place in their intimacy, and the Sexperiment will get you into the habit of regular, consistent, intentional intimacy, which is a building block of oneness.

Sex is an anchor in marriage because there's only one person with whom you engage in this special expression of intimacy. It's the superglue that sanctifies marriage. It sets you and your spouse apart from everything else. You could share space with a person you're not married to. You can share meals with a person you're not married to. You could share finances with a person you're not married to. You can feel love for a person you're not married to. You could share your deepest feelings and secrets with a person you're not married to. You could even parent with a person you're not married to; divorced couples do it all the time. But the act of sexual intercourse—in God's economy—is reserved exclusively for husbands and wives. Sexual intimacy is the bonding agent God wants only married couples to experience, because it is something that goes beyond any other bond we have.

The Benefits

A while back, an Internet poll was conducted among 60,000 fathers. Of the men surveyed, 79 percent of them said that they wanted more sex. Then, 60 percent of these guys said that they regularly view porn. Beyond that, 40 percent of these fathers shared that their sexual advances are rejected at least once a week.* Isn't that amazing?

According to the survey results, by a wide margin, fathers (and probably mothers, too) do not feel as though they are experiencing one of the major benefits of marriage as much as they ought to or want to. An active, healthy sex life within the context of marriage has many benefits to couples.

Some spouses do say that sex isn't really important to them. In some cases that's true. However, the overwhelming majority of spouses will categorically say that sex matters to their marriage and that they're not getting it enough.

Regular sex will deepen your marriage, because it's an outward reflection of an inward connection. The more you have sex, the more you're saying emotionally, physically, and spiritually, "We are one. We're connected." As you engage in the Sexperiment, you will get in touch and connect with seven benefits of sexual intimacy in marriage (we'll unpack these more throughout the pages of the book, but this is just a quick glance).

Sexual intimacy in marriage fulfills God's purpose.

When married couples make love, they are living out the fulfillment of God's plan for marriage. A regular, healthy sex life helps you to become one with your spouse. God created sex as a bond for recreation and for procreation in marriage. He wants married couples to enjoy each other sexually, and also to have children and raise them in love.

Sexual intimacy in marriage reveals our true self.

The very nature of sexual intimacy is revealing. Sex requires a level of intimacy, oneness, and openness that only married couples

---

* http://www.inquisitr.com/4103/poll-reveals-32-of-dads-had-affair-since-having-children -jessica-alba-tops-dads-sexual-fantasies/

should have. The Bible tells us that when we have sex with someone, we become one with them.* When sexual intimacy takes place, we're emotionally naked, we're spiritually naked, and we're physically naked. Nakedness assumes intimacy. In your week of the Sexperiment, you will experience new opportunities to be open and vulnerable with your spouse. And you'll experience the strength that develops with those new opportunities.

Sexual intimacy in marriage thwarts sexual temptation.

Every time you think about temptation, you've got to think about your purpose. Temptation is all about getting us *off* purpose. Greater sexual intimacy with our spouse makes us accountable to each other as husband and wife. It also fulfills a very real physical need, which makes us less vulnerable to temptation outside the marriage bed. Put simply, if you're having it at home, you'll be less likely to be tempted to look for it somewhere else!

Sexual intimacy in marriage establishes a legacy.

The greatest legacy you can leave, the greatest influence you can have on your kids is to make love regularly. When you have a regular, healthy sex life with your spouse, you can even affect the people you work with if you want to snap the heads of others who will say, "Something is different about your life and about your marriage." And it opens up the opportunities to share with others about God's purpose and plan for our lives.

In marriage, as the sexual intimacy goes, so goes evidence of forgiveness, communication skills, and so many other areas of importance. Our children see all of that modeled in how we treat each other and how we relate to each other. Now, they don't see the sacredness of our bedroom, but they know that we have that intimacy because it is reflected in all the different areas outside the bedroom as well.

---

* 1 Corinthians 6:16

We're leaving a legacy because when our children select a spouse, they're going to be thinking so deeply about that relationship and what it means and what it stands for. After they marry, they will have a benchmark by which to judge the romance, the creativity, the love, and the spiritual leadership that they should be looking for.

Leave a legacy for your kids, their future spouses, your grand-children. Allow them to see how you have made your spouse and your marriage a priority.

Sexual intimacy in marriage helps us bring our best.

Maybe you've seen the commercial for an erectile dysfunction medication where the guy comes to work and people can tell there's something different about him, but they can't quite figure it out. The message is the man's being fulfilled through a regular sex life and it's showing in every other part of his life as well. That's the power of sexual intimacy.

The amount of sexual activity a couple has is definitely a barom-eter reading of their marriage. In order to have regular sex, both spouses have to bring their best—kindness, courtesy, concern for the other's needs, unselfishness. When these qualities are expressed, it motivates us to be intimate, but it also creates benefits in every other area of the relationship.

When you make love regularly, it forces you to come to terms with issues such as forgiveness, which has a huge effect on every other aspect of your relationship. Every marriage deals with the same stuff, but the successful marriages negotiate around those bar-riers and deal with them.

Sexual intimacy in marriage helps us
concentrate on our spouse.

Marriage is all about unselfishness. It is about the other person. Whenever Lisa and I have problems in our marriage—and believe me, we do—I take the stance that I'm to blame. Often, I'm tempted to say, "But Lisa is not doing this, and she's doing this." It can be easy to point my finger and direct the blame. But the reality is that God calls me to work only on my problems and how I can work to resolve any issue in the marriage. Guys, even if you are only 0.0001 percent wrong, it is your responsibility to step up and make it right. We can point fingers all day, but the bottom line is, I have to change before God what I can change and leave the rest up to Him.

It is easy to look at the faults of someone else and see what is wrong with them and not pay attention to yourself. But in marriage, we have to put our spouse's needs above our own. We can't let that old points system take control of our minds and start thinking, "Well, but he didn't consider me at this place or here in this area."

Couples say marriage should be 50/50. But God's way is 100/100. The points system makes us say things like, "Well, if he only gave forty percent, then I'll only give forty percent." But that is not what Christ did for us. He gave 100 percent of himself, and marriage is a reflection of Christ and the church. He gave himself up for the church and we should express that kind of sacrificial, 100 percent, giving-to-each-other kind of love. Marriage is all about fulfilling the needs and serving the needs of the other.

Sexual intimacy in marriage cultivates creativity.

You may already have been thinking about how you and your spouse can keep your lovemaking exciting for seven straight days, and even beyond. The Sexperiment, and a consistent sex life, is not about completing a task. It is about a deeper meaning—loving each other in a more significant way and a more creative way. The Sexperiment has helped Lisa and me think more creatively about romance and about how to spice up our love life.

Creativity doesn't have to cost much, and it doesn't have to be highly detailed or elaborate. But it does take a commitment and willingness to find new ways to keep intimacy alive in your marriage.

When our kids were younger, after we put them to bed, we would occasionally have a candlelight picnic in our bedroom. That was the romance and the creativity part for us during those days.

Creativity is simply finding small ways to tweak your routine that will help keep energy and vitality in the marriage. During this Sexperiment, you'll begin to think of new ways to do what you already want to do!

Practice, Patience, and Persistence

I love to fly-fish, and any fly fisherman worth his salt makes his own flies. We call it fly tying. I can see some similarities between tying flies and the oneness couples experience in marriage. (It's a guy thing, ladies.) To be good at fly tying, it takes practice, patience, and persistence. That's definitely true in marriage. Oneness requires practice, patience, and persistence.

Oneness comes through practice. All couples make mistakes along their journey toward oneness. That's why the Bible tells us that we "become" one flesh; it doesn't say we are immediately one flesh once we're married.

So you make your mistakes, seek forgiveness, and do better the next time. That's *practice*. Then that same spouse tries to do better, but messes up again. You grant forgiveness (again). That's *patience*. There's some trial and error involved in marriage, so you need *persistence* to continue the becoming process.

Let's face it; some spouses are A students when it comes to doing the things necessary to become one. Others have arrested development. Some couples grow toward oneness with finesse, like swans on the lake. Others grow through the-bull-in-the-china-shop method: after surveying the collateral damage all around them, they realize that they are in it together, and they grow more toward oneness.

The first time I tied a fly, it wasn't very pretty. But after some repeated effort, I got much better at it. Early in marriage, our efforts toward oneness may be clumsy. There may even be times when things don't look very hopeful for the marriage. But don't despair. Giving that repeated effort will definitely help things to get better!

After I mastered the technique to tie one type of fly, I decided it was time to try another type. I did better than the first time I ever tied one, but I still needed practice, patience, and persistence to learn each new fly pattern. It's the same with growing in oneness.

We get one area of marital oneness down, but then there are others to cultivate and learn. It's a process. Maybe the financial oneness in your marriage is a solid rock. Then you improve every year in the area of mutual submission. You become one in your understanding of the roles of a husband and a wife. Next you're rock solid in oneness regarding parenting.

I've known couples who have all the other areas of marital oneness in place except the sexual component. I think that's why so many couples have been pleasantly amazed by the results they've gotten from participating in the Sexperiment, even though the formula behind it is pretty simple: more sex, more intimacy; less sex, less intimacy.

Too many couples are living with less intimacy. They tell themselves things like, "Sex isn't everything. We've got all these other things going for us." I'm always amazed to hear about couples who have gone months and even years without being intimate.

It's great when those other areas of marriage come together, because they're important. But couples need to focus on sexual intimacy as much as those other aspects. It's the bond, just like superglue is the bond that holds a fishing fly together. You see, you can expertly assemble a fly. It can even be beautiful, but you have to have a way to secure the thread ends after you tie it off. You need superglue to hold it all together. Sex in marriage holds the bond together, like superglue.

Now, I'm not naïve. I realize that people marry for all sorts of reasons—financial security, status, loneliness, biological clock ticking. There's an old saying: "When you marry for money, you'll earn every penny." It's good to have things like financial security and companionship in marriage, but these components are not enough to establish a lifelong bond.

Marriage, God's way, according to His design, calls for oneness in every area of the relationship. That includes sex. If you fail to focus on the sexual-intimacy side, you're falling victim to fractional thinking, not wholeness thinking. Many, many couples go through life united in fractional marriages when God's design for marriage is wholeness.

Wholeness and holiness in marriage reflect the gospel message of Jesus Christ—his death, burial, and resurrection. Through our marriages, people should see reconciliation. They should see unconditional love. They should see unselfishness. They should also see a couple who are intimate and loving. Husbands and wives have an opportunity, through the platform of marriage, to demonstrate the love of Christ to each other and to the world.

As a pastor, the greatest sermon I will ever preach is the way I treat Lisa. If I speak eloquently to the church, but speak harshly to my best friend, I have invalidated the Word of God in my own life. And I've cheapened the power of the good news that Christ has lived, died, and risen again for my sins.

The same is true in your marriage. You may not be a pastor, but you can tell people about God's love through your marriage. If you read the Bible for two hours a day but are constantly ignoring your spouse's needs, it won't do much good for your marriage or your Christian testimony. If you are damaging your spouse with the words you speak, the words you communicate to God won't go very far.

Through the Sexperiment, you begin to put the work into your marriage that makes it a living testimony about the wholeness and holiness of God. Through your physical intimacy, you will discover how your marriage becomes a place of worship to the Lord.

Security in Marriage

When our twins were young, I remember holding their little hands as we walked across the street. I would grab each twin's hand and hold it tightly. They would always try to break free of my grasp, but I wasn't letting go. No matter how much they tried, they couldn't break away, because I had a vise grip on their little hands. I didn't want them to run into oncoming traffic.

Once we invite Christ into our lives, our heavenly Father grabs our hands. He's not going to let us go. He's not going to divorce us, and we can't divorce Him. He's not going to turn His back on us, no matter what. We can't get out of His family. Once you're in, you're in. Theologians call it "the security of the believer." As a believer in Christ, I'm secure in knowing there's nothing I can do to cause God to stop loving me.

We should have that same kind of security in marriage. The security that Lisa and I have in our marriage should be reflective of the security that we have in Christ. And when you have that kind of security, come hell or high water, you're going to stay married. When you are determined that you will stay together no matter what, you have confidence in your spouse and in your marriage. You're sure of yourself in marriage. You know that you have an agenda above and beyond this world. There is nothing like security in marriage.

Security in marriage builds oneness and intimacy, especially for wives, because women have a high need to feel secure in the relationship. Husbands, your wife needs to know that you're not going to abandon her after a few years or in the midst of a midlife crisis. She needs to know that you're not going to be flipping through the *Sports Illustrated* Swimsuit Edition when her waistline expands during pregnancy. As her husband, only you can give her that feeling of security.

But men need to feel secure about certain things too. Wives, your husband needs to know that you will not ridicule him or put him down if he loses his job. He needs to know that you trust him to be the leader of your home. A man's lack of security about being desired by his wife often may move him to stray to the wrong bed. This is a frequent male response to the perception that he isn't wanted at home. (However, many men also aren't doing the things that cause them to be wanted.) Men will go where they are wanted.

I'm certainly not giving men a pass on this or creating excuses. I'm simply stating what so many men/husbands have shared with me. Security in marriage, on the part of both spouses, helps to build oneness. And oneness builds intimacy that expresses itself through an amazing level of physical closeness.

The high rate of divorce, even among Christians, doesn't give us a lot of reasons to feel secure in marriage. We've all known couples that divorce and we think, "No, not you guys! I thought your marriage was rock solid!"

Every year, people marry in elaborate church ceremonies and settings and divorce before the wedding is paid for. Some of the wedding gifts haven't even been used before the divorce is final!

Developing the level of security in marriage that supports oneness is intentional and deliberate. For example, Lisa and I have given each other ten marital commandments to guide our conduct within marriage. These commandments, coupled with our wedding vows, give us both a sense of security in marriage that helps strengthen our oneness. We have allowed God to determine what's important to us, and then created our "commandments" from there.

10 Commandments of Oneness*

1. I shall have no other human relationship before Lisa/Ed.
2. Remember date night and keep it holy.
3. Honor Lisa/Ed on anniversaries and special days so that I may live long in the land the Lord has given me.
4. I shall not take the covenant of marriage in vain.
5. I shall not ride in a car or eat in a restaurant alone with a member of the opposite sex.

---

*NOTE: Lisa and I put these commandments together as they relate to our lives. We suggest that you, as a couple, use these and make the needed adjustments for your life. The most important thing is to write them and live by them.

6. I shall not travel alone.
7. I shall not counsel with a member of the opposite sex alone behind closed doors.
8. I shall not share the details of my marriage with others.
9. I shall not watch, read, or expose myself to sexually explicit shows, books, websites, etc.
10. I shall remember the implications of committing adultery.

God wants the marital relationship to validate the claims of Christianity to a watching world. He wants marriage to be an example of Christ's redeeming love, overcoming the vices and the effects of sin. But it can be challenging. Between what we read in magazines and on the Internet and what we see on television and at the movies, many people have a pretty confused and distorted idea of what marriage is and is supposed to be. Adult children from divorced or single-parent households want to marry and have a fulfilling, stable family life, yet they have no earthly idea what marriage is really all about.

The world is dying to see true, authentic, high-definition marriages. The world is dying to see high-definition love, high-definition forgiveness, and high-definition unselfishness. Where are they going to see it? They will see it in our marriage and yours and that of every other couple who puts Christ at the center of their marriage. But they can't see it in us unless we commit ourselves to the level of intimacy that the Sexperiment is designed to lead us toward.

Culture Clash: Covenant vs. Contract

If I'm going to be the kind of husband that I should be before God, and if Lisa is going to be the kind of wife that she should be before God, there has to be a death in our marriage. It's not the kind of death that guys joke about when one of them gets married.

No, it's a different kind of death. We have to "die to self" in marriage. That's a difficult phrase for our culture to grasp. But basically, we have to bury our baggage, our selfishness, our issues, and yield to the flow of God's resurrection power, which is always on tap. We have to let that power flow into our lives so that together we can become the kind of difference makers together that God desires. It's all about being connected in partnership as one, but not the way our culture sees partnership.

We live in a contract-crazy culture, don't we? You have to sign a contract to do almost anything. If you want a cell phone, a lot of companies still want you to sign a contract. If you want satellite or cable television, you sign a contract. If you want to lease a car, rent an apartment, or buy a home, you sign a contract. If you want to get married, you sign a contract. But how good are contracts?

Contracts are unique because, basically, they say, "If you keep your end of the deal, I'll keep mine. But the moment I don't feel like you're keeping your end, I'm out. I no longer have an obligation to fulfill my end. I can rip the contract up."

That's how contracts work. If the landlord violates the lease, I don't have to live there and pay rent until the contract ends.

That's the problem with so many marriages. They don't make it because any excuse to bail on the relationship will do. Our contract-obsessed culture is a whirlwind of affidavits and stipulations and fine print and prenups. We see everything as a contract, as if it is our guarantee of equity.

What is a contract? Let me give you the definition. There are two of them, according to the dictionary:

1. A binding agreement between two or more persons or parties.
2. A business arrangement for the supply of goods or services at a fixed price.

When we regard marriage as a contract, we've doomed it from the start. A contract is more about what you cannot do, so it emphasizes the negative. This "contract" approach to marriage is one of the reasons why it is so simple to get a divorce. We can just call our lawyers and let them pick up the pieces. That's what happens with a contract. A *covenant,* on the other hand, which is how God designed marriage, is entirely different.

When we go to a wedding, what are we thinking about? "I wonder how much this thing cost."

"Wow, she must have lost about twenty pounds to fit into that dress, didn't she?"

"Have you seen her ring? That thing is huge!"

"Oh, girl, I would never use those colors! Those are hideous!"

That's what we're thinking about during the ceremony. But let's think deeper. The wedding is not just a ceremony followed by a big party. A wedding is a ceremony that symbolizes a covenant. When a man and a woman become husband and wife before God and some family and friends, they are cutting a covenant. It's a blood bond of life and death. Some of you are thinking, "You mean, we did that when we got married? I didn't realize all that was going on! I must have been really nervous."

But that's exactly what you did. During the wedding ceremony, you and your spouse, like Lisa and me, made a covenant—a blood bond of life and death.

In our modern-day vernacular, we can say that a covenant is a commitment on steroids. The word *covenant* is used 286 times throughout the Bible. All you have to do is thumb through the Scriptures and you'll see this word over and over. God was always making covenants with his people. One of the major covenants God made was with a guy named Abram, also known as Abraham. One day God told him, "Leave your country, your people and your father's household and go to the land I will show you..."*

Abraham was rich beyond rich. He was a squillionaire! When God told him to move, it was a major deal. Don't think about a mom and a dad and 2.3 kids and maybe a dog and a cat moving from Dallas

---

* Genesis 12:1–3

to Seattle. Think Bill Gates. Think of a Fortune 500 company moving from one country to another country. This guy, who had megabucks, was commissioned by God to move to a new tract of land, the ultimate piece of real estate: Canaan.

Then God made Abraham a serious offer that was too good for him to pass up. God said, "I will make you into a great nation and I will bless you. I will make your name great, and you will be a blessing. I will bless those who bless you, and whoever curses you I will curse; and all peoples on earth will be blessed through you."

But when all God's promises didn't come together right away, Abraham came back and asked a question that we all ask God sometimes. God had told him to move, and he did. Once he was on the move, he asked, in essence, "God, how can I know for sure that I'm going to get what you promised?"*

God responded to him with a covenant. He made a covenant with Abraham and said, "To your descendants I give this land."†

The original Hebrew word "covenant" comes from a phrase meaning "to cut." So Abraham brought a cow, a goat, and a ram (this is going to be kind of gross) and split them in two. He arranged the bloody halves opposite each other. Then God passed through the bloody pieces of the animals' carcasses, thus taking the initiative in the covenant.

God said, "I'm going to pour out my supernatural favor on your life. I'm going to bless you. I love you unconditionally. I'm going to make your name great and you're going to make a huge difference in the world. I'm going to keep my end of the deal. I'm in covenant with you."

Another important covenant in the Bible is between two friends, Jonathan and David. The Bible says, "Jonathan made a covenant with David because he loved him as himself. Jonathan took off the robe he was wearing and gave it to David, along with his tunic, and even his

---

* Genesis 15:8
† Genesis 15:18

sword, his bow and his belt."* David and Jonathan exchanged robes to demonstrate their becoming one. They exchanged belts, and this illustrated the fact that they were helping each other with their weaknesses. Their weapons exchange symbolized that they were going to fight each other's enemies. Then they took an animal and, you guessed it, cut it down the middle, arranged the halves opposite each other, stood back-to-back, and walked through the bloody animal halves in a figure eight, illustrating the eternal nature of the covenant.

In their covenant, they were saying, "God, if we break this covenant, you do to us what we did to these animals." So that portion of the covenant was called the "walk of death." After the walk of death, they took each other's names and made a public pronouncement: "Hey, we're in covenant together, a blood bond of life and death." Then they shared a covenant meal.

The fact that they called it the "walk of death" lets us know the seriousness of the covenant. They were saying, "I am dying to self. I'm in this thing for life. I don't care what happens. If you're broke, busted, and disgusted, come hell or high water, I'm in it for life because this thing we're doing is before God. I'm committing myself to you— no matter what—warts and all. Self-centered, imperfect and all, I'm giving my life to you before God."

Covenant marriage is all about surrendering the self. When the apostle Paul told the Christians in Ephesus to "submit to one another out of reverence for Christ," he was talking to both spouses.† Covenant marriage is all about submission. I've submitted myself, my needs, and my agenda to God and to Lisa. And she has done the same to God and to me.

During the Sexperiment, you will engage in the process of mutual submission. You are submitting your bodies, your desires, and your needs to each other. Even if your schedule gets hectic or you're up really late during your challenge week, remember that it's

---

* 1 Samuel 18 3–4
† Ephesians 5:21

all about submission. I can tell you that you will experience a new level of joy and fulfillment from submission. Your actions will not only be pleasing to your spouse, but also pleasing to God.

If we allow the covenant to govern us in marriage, we'll find ourselves doing positive things we normally wouldn't do, saying kind things we normally wouldn't say, and acting out courtesies we normally wouldn't act out. It's the influence of covenant love.

One time, a friend invited Lisa and me to this fabulous resort and we hung out there for several hours. We were lying out in the sun, and beautiful people were at this resort with yachts. It was the jet-set club. And I was wearing these wraparound black sunglasses. No one could see my eyes. Well, this friend wanted Lisa and me to meet some of her friends, so she called to a lady who was walking down the beach. And this lady turned and began to walk toward us. This girl was a real show-stopper! She would embarrass any Victoria's Secret model. She was wearing a bikini that was made of less cotton than is in an aspirin bottle.

I'm sure you're wondering what was going through my mind as I saw this woman approaching. Well, it was the perfect setup, because I'm a normal red-blooded guy. So I was thinking, "Wow! Unbelievable!" I didn't say those words out loud, though (I'm pretty smart).

What do you do when you have a scenario like that? Do you simply appreciate the beauty? Or do you go to a place called Lust Vegas? (We'll talk about that place more in a later chapter.) In a case like that, you can't say, "It's about me and what I like," because you're in a covenant relationship that's about oneness.

Covenant marriage is about "us." When I talk about lust, it has to be about us—Lisa and me—because it affects us. So what did I do about the beautiful woman? I honored our covenant with my eyes. I took my sunglasses off. I wanted Lisa to see my eyes. I wanted this young lady to see my eyes. I looked her in the eyes. Obviously, I saw that she was beautiful. I felt the tug, the pull toward temptation. But I thought to myself, "You know what? My body is God's. My body is Lisa's. I'm not going down that path. I'm going to honor our covenant and put Lisa first."

When we choose to stay within the safety and security of covenant, we grow in oneness because we make it more important than any fleeting human feelings, desires, or emotions.

Potholes in the Road to Oneness

The road to oneness is seldom smooth every day or all the way. There are a lot of potholes in the road to oneness. I have hit a few of them and so have you, and they'll keep coming. But if you keep Christ first, at the center of your marriage, he will fill the potholes and smooth the rough places.

As Christ followers, a husband and wife are not one flesh only through marriage, but they are also one in Christ. God has spoken clearly through His Word that some serious oneness should be taking place within a Christian marriage. You can't say, "Well, it's his problem" about your husband or "It's her problem" about your wife. No, it is *our* problem.

Peter, one of Jesus's disciples, said, "All of you be of one mind."* Then Peter said, "Having compassion for one another, be tenderhearted, be courteous."

The word *courteous* has the word "court" in it. When you are courteous toward your spouse, you are courting him or her. What do you do, for example, when your spouse does a chore around the house? Hopefully your first reaction isn't "You missed a spot!" It should be words of appreciation. When you get up early and raise the thermostat so the house will be warm when your spouse gets out of bed, that's being courteous.

But the reverse is also true. When I am critical of Lisa or she is critical of me, we are, in fact, criticizing ourselves, because we are one. It should not be a relationship of dissonance but of harmony. In our egotistical, me-centered world, our society has a tough time with

---

* 1 Peter 3:8, NKJV

the concept of harmony and oneness in relationships. The competitive one-upmanship that is so pervasive in our culture should never find its way into the marital scheme, because our criticisms and judgments hardly ever serve to build up the other person. Instead, people tend to use criticisms as ammunition to make themselves look better by putting down the other person. But the apostle Paul says that our speech should be "helpful for building others up according to their needs, that it may benefit those who listen."*

When critique (criticism) is warranted, it should be given in a timely and respectful manner. The ultimate goal of criticism is to improve and enhance the situation, not tear it down. Each of us should be receptive to timely critique. But we should be much more generous with courteous words (encouragement) than words of criticism.

Are you measuring your words to your spouse according to his or her needs? Or do you sometimes spout off selective psychobabble to meet your own perceived need to feel better and make them feel worse? Skip the psychobabble and concentrate on those crucial words, phrases, and conversations that will build you both up as one flesh.

In a sense, the Sexperiment is a natural tool for helping you in the building-up process. The kind of intimacy that the challenge draws out of you requires you to relate to each other courteously and compassionately, or you won't be successful at it. Think about it: You will hardly be motivated to intimacy if you are in an angry, hostile, or unforgiving mode toward each other. Sexual intimacy requires submission, compassion, and all the words and behaviors that help you to build the other up.

Before you begin the challenge, try a visual exercise to help you see where you're trying to go as a couple. Try the salt covenant. Some couples have incorporated the salt covenant as a part of their wedding ceremony. This symbol of covenant is based on Numbers 18:19 and 2 Chronicles 13:5.

---

* Ephesians 4:29

During the marriage ceremony, both the groom and the bride take a small amount of salt in their hands. Both can pour their salt into a single vial and establish that the covenant can only be broken if both parties can find and separate each grain of salt they put in. Some couples throw their handful of salt upward into the wind. As the salt is blown away and eventually lands, the covenant is established. They can be released from the marriage covenant only if they are able to retrieve every grain of salt that was cast into the wind. Trying this with your spouse can help you make a visual connection to the oneness you're hoping to achieve.

That is what happens when people come together in marriage. God says there will be so much trust, love, vulnerability, and commitment in this one-flesh relationship that it will be the greatest human relationship in the world. And when you follow His plan for your marriage, it will be impossible to undo it.

Action Steps

1. Recall and recite your wedding vows regularly (once a month, during a date night).

2. Use the Ten Commandments of Oneness as a foundation to create your own set of commandments for building oneness in your marriage. Ask yourselves, "Is our marriage a contract or a covenant?" Determine one sacrificial act that you can do to demonstrate to your spouse the covenantal nature of your marriage.

3. You and your spouse create a separate listing of areas in your marriage where you have achieved oneness. Compare lists to see if you agree. Compliment your spouse for the willingness and patience to work toward oneness in those specific areas. Discuss areas of your marriage where you knowingly have both achieved oneness. Talk about how you can build on those successes to build oneness in the areas where you still have work to do.

4. Both spouses should ask, "Do I feel secure in our marriage?" Share the components of your marriage that affirm your feelings of security. Then discuss the potholes you have hit on the road to oneness in your marriage and how they were overcome.

5. Write down how you believe seven days of sex can further your marriage along the journey of oneness.

6. Perform your own salt covenant as a symbol of your commitment to the covenantal foundation of your marriage.

———— *Before You Do* ————

*R*ight now, the process of becoming one seems romantic. You probably can't wait to get there. But understand that oneness is a process that begins after the vows are taken. It's not a done deal just because you say "I do."

Maybe you plan to have a unity candle in your wedding ceremony. With a unity candle, you usually have three candles on a candelabra—two on the outside and then one in the middle. The one in the middle is not lit. The two candles on either side are lit and then the bride and groom take their lit candles and light the one in the middle. Then the bride and groom blow out their own candles. Lighting the unity candle is a symbolic act to say, "As I join with you, I surrender my stuff, my feelings, my desires, my needs so that we can become one."

Think about whether you're ready to do more than just carry out a symbolic act in a ceremony. Are you willing to do what it takes to become one—to die to self in order to achieve oneness in the covenant bond of marriage?

Do you have some area of your life that will be off-limits to your future spouse? Look inward and assess whether you're already planning for divorce by devising ways to keep separateness in the relationship after you marry.

The Yoke Is Not a Joke

*T*he Old Testament prophet Amos asked, "Can two people walk together without agreeing on the direction?"* Two people going in opposite directions cannot become one. That is why God wants Christians to be equally yoked in marriage with other Christians. God wants to spare us the pain and agony of being hooked up with someone with whom we can never achieve oneness. His desire for us is to unite in covenant with a mate who will model the love of Christ. God created marriage to be an institution in which and through which we can thrive and grow closer to Him.

If you make a love connection with someone who is not using the same owner's manual as you, the relationship is headed for serious trouble. Don't use a "showroom mentality" while dating. Car dealers will tell you that when men and women think about buying a car, they walk into the showroom, look at the lines of the body, and focus on a few features of the car. Most of them will buy that car within twenty-four to forty-eight hours. They make a quick decision based on a few features. That's the showroom mentality. Look deeply at the whole person, not just a few attractive features, to determine your capacity to develop oneness with him or her.

Dating is all about finding the *ulti-mate*. No matter how casual, no matter how platonic, every person you spend time with is someone about whom you likely will ask the question "Could this be the one?" Whether that person is or isn't "the one," connect with other Christ followers, even in dating. You will never reach your ulti-mate destination unless you are equally joined in Christ. So why not do it from the start?

---

* Amos 3:3, NLT

4

It's Time to Get Naked

One of the greatest compliments Lisa and I have ever received happened while we were out of town. Each day of the trip, we would walk by a set of shops near the hotel where we were staying. One of those shops was a little jewelry store. Each day we would walk in, look around, and talk with the store's owner. Eventually, he found out that I am a pastor. Near the end of the week, he stopped us and said, "I want to tell you something. Whatever you're preaching, I know it's real because your marriage is real. You guys truly love each other. I can tell just by the way you treat each other."

When we walked out of the store that day, Lisa and I told each other, "Is that incredible?! We're not perfect. But somehow, this man saw God in the way we treat each other. I think that is the greatest compliment we've ever received!"

What did this man see in our marriage? In Lisa and me? I believe that he saw the culmination of many years of working toward openness and intimacy in marriage. Lisa and I are completely open and intimate within our marriage. But I believe the store owner saw the public manifestation of the private intimacy in our marriage. Lisa and I are committed to each other, but every now and then it's nice to have someone else notice that our commitment is real and true. It's the greatest testimony I have as a pastor, as a Christian, and as a husband. When you're completely open and intimate with each other in private, that openness transcends every aspect of your relationship.

Nakedness is a gift that God has given humankind. Animals can't get naked. Our Doberman does not say, "Oh, turn your head! Let me get my gym shorts on before you look at me!" The little dogs that we dress up in cute little outfits don't care about those clothes. In fact, most of the time, they can't wait to take them off.

The first man and woman God created were naked.* Adam wasn't made by God wearing an Armani suit, and Eve wasn't fashioned by God wearing five-inch Jimmy Choo heels. They were naked, but not just physically. They were naked emotionally and spiritually.

The Bible says that the first man and woman God created were both naked and they were not ashamed. Now, that's interesting, because most people want to cover their nakedness if they have no clothes on. That's why we wear clothes. Yet Adam and Eve felt no shame. Why? Because they were united in a bond of marriage. Their nakedness transcended their physical state. They had nothing hidden or concealed from each other or from God. It was only when sin entered in that they felt ashamed. Sin makes us feel ashamed.

God's design is for us to be naked in marriage. Don't worry; I'm not suggesting that couples walk around physically naked 24/7. Nakedness assumes openness, with no barriers to intimacy and trust. What does intimacy mean? It means to be fully known. In marriage, we're to get naked physically, emotionally, spiritually, economically, and psychologically so that we can be fully known by each other.

The Sexperiment is a venture into nakedness—the kind of openness and vulnerability that are essential to true intimacy in marriage. Nakedness happens within the covenant of marriage.

Millions of people have crossed the line by getting naked with someone outside the boundaries of marriage. The Bible says repeatedly that we're not to take sex out of context. We're not to make big

---

* Genesis 2:25

sex (in the context of marriage) into little sex (premarital or extra-marital affairs).

There are two options when it comes to having sex. You either have big sex or you have little sex. Think of it as the big bed or the little bed. In our house, the little beds are reserved for the dogs. People don't sleep there. But that's what sex outside of marriage is doing. It's taking sex out of the big bed of marriage and putting it into the little dog bed and saying, "I can't help it. I know what God wants for me to do with sex. I know he's reserved it for marriage. But I'm just an animal. I can't help but do it whenever, wherever, and with whomever. I'm a deer in rut, a hound in heat."

But when we take the content (sex) out of the context (marriage), there's only one result: chaos. The truth is that we aren't animals. We're not hounds in heat or deer in rut. We're people, designed in the image of God. And God doesn't want us to experience little sex in the dog bed; he wants us to experience the power and purpose of big sex in the right bed.

Big sex happens in the marriage bed. Little sex happens outside the marriage bed. We're not to minimize or trivialize sex or reduce it to a physical act that fills a need, like eating when we're hungry. We're to keep sex in the big bed—reserved for marriage only.

How do we keep sex big? We do it God's way by trusting Him. If you're married, you trust God. If you're a single adult, you trust God. If you're about to be married, you trust God.

If we get out of the big bed, and get into the little bed of sexual sin, the repercussions are so far-reaching that it's difficult to understand them all. It doesn't take a neuroscientist to see that our world is facing all kinds of diseases, brokenness, and confusion. And a huge chunk of that is due to sexual sin—using sex outside of God's design for it. I've talked to a lot of people about sin, because after all, sin is my business. I've talked to people who are involved in drugs. I've talked to people who have taken another person's life. I've talked to people who have robbed and engaged in all kinds of sin. But after all the conversations I've had with people about their sin, I'm convinced there is no sin like sexual sin, because the sexual nerve is woven into the very depth of who we are.

Our culture says sex is no big deal. But it is a big deal; it's a huge deal! God made it big and we keep it big by honoring it as the glorious act of worship that God intended it to be. When sexual intercourse happens between a husband and a wife, it is a reflection of the nature and character of God. The feminine aspects of God join with the masculine aspects to become one.

Sex is not just a physical act. It's a soulish thing. It's a Trinitarian thing—a part of our mind, a part of our body, and a part of our spirit. We can't get away from it. Yet people say, "Hey, we're just going to have sex."

"Friends with benefits," they call it. And they think they can park their souls outside the bedroom and just have sex. Well, it doesn't work that way, because there's no such thing as "just sex." I think women tend to grasp this concept more quickly than men because the act of sexual intercourse involves actually entering a woman's body. They tend to understand the significance of having someone enter their body. Very often men don't get it as quickly: Sex is not just a physical thing.

If you and your spouse engaged in premarital sex, after you got married you discovered something. The sexual rules changed. In marriage, great sex is based on nonsexual things—romance, intimacy, conversation, environment. But you don't really find that out until after you get married. Furthermore, when you involve yourself in premarital sex, it is so powerful that it can cloud your head and distract you from the nonsexual stuff that you should be working on prior to marriage. And now that you're married, because you didn't work on the nonsexual stuff, your attempts to connect sexually can get a bit awkward. You realize now, "Uh-oh, now sex is about a lot of nonsexual stuff."

The nonsexual stuff is about work. It's about getting open and vulnerable and naked. It's hard for a lot of guys to get emotionally naked, so we have a lot of men moving to pornography and lust. I may have to give up my man card for this one, but a lot of guys simply don't want to do the work that true intimacy requires. They don't want to communicate, so they sit down and channel surf for breasts and body parts, or they go to kennel clubs and watch as women perform for them, or they live and feed on lust and have extramarital relationships.

Why do they do it? Why would they trade something as beautiful and special as true intimacy for something as common and uncreative as porn or lust? They do it because, let's face it, it's easy.

Sometimes true intimacy is lacking because husbands and wives are unknowingly making assumptions. Take, for instance, a man who is a good provider for his family and that is how he demonstrates his love. But maybe there's something missing. His wife may not share his feelings of intimacy and he wonders why. That man may say, "I don't understand why she's not happy. She doesn't have to work. She has a nice new car, a nice house, and credit cards to buy whatever she wants."

But what the wife may be longing for is not material. What she's missing is authentic intimacy and true vulnerability from her husband in every other area. Sex, for women, begins long before they enter the bedroom. It begins with things like kindness, communication, touch without an agenda. Understanding her needs is a giant step toward oneness, just as a wife understanding her husband's needs is a major move in the direction of oneness.

Intimacy Blockers

There are just some issues that can absolutely hinder openness and intimacy in marriage, and if they're present in your marriage don't be surprised when they surface during your week of the Sexperiment. Pornography, lust, masturbation, infidelity, unforgiveness, and any kind of abuse keep intimacy confined and contained in marriage. There are people who believe that porn, lust, and masturbation are aids to intimacy, but in reality they do nothing to promote openness, intimacy, or oneness in marriage. If any of those things are happening in your marriage, you may have a certain level of intimacy but you won't experience the deep level of openness that is the ultimate in marriage.

Pornography

Some people have actually said that pornography is good for a marriage. Having counseled many, many couples over the years, I can tell you that this is simply not true. It's never true. Maybe it helps an unsaved couple because it's something they agree on, something they share. Maybe. But in a marriage of believers, you cannot achieve greater intimacy through pornography. A husband and wife who see sex and marriage as God sees it also see the math of marriage as $1 + 1 = 1$. There is no room there for a third party. Pornography is a third party. Marriage and pornography don't go together. One simple reason why is because one spouse is usually into it, but not the other. Porn is often one spouse's secret that serves no purpose other than to keep couples from coming to true vulnerability and nakedness. It keeps the spouse who looks at it wrapped up in a fantasy world of perfect body parts.

Pornography impedes nakedness, openness, and intimacy because it is all about illusion. Specifically, it is all about the illusion of intimacy. Pornography says, "Yeah, you can feel and experience intimacy without making a personal investment." That is a lie.

What does pornography really do? Pornography strips sex and nakedness of its God-designed significance. It takes sex out of the context and purpose for which it was intended. Pornography is also very selfish. It's so tempting for men because the typical man thinks, "I don't have to work or think or risk. I'll just make myself feel good with the help of all these airbrushed images that are available 24/7. Those women never nag. They never have a headache. They're never too tied up with the kids. They're always willing, always smiling, and always there and in the mood."

Watching porn is self-centered. It's just about *you*, because you can surf, you can change the channels, you can rent the video, and you can go to the strip clubs. And while you're watching strippers, you're stripping the women and yourself of their humanity. Using people as products is not God's way. It's just about lust.

Lust

When we get hooked on lust, we begin to fight and we hurt innocent bystanders—spouses, children, friends, and careers. Then Satan reels us in. But Satan does not practice catch and release. He keeps every person he catches as a trophy. And sadly, his trophy room is full of prey. There is a strategy right now that the Evil One has for your life and mine to mess us up with lust. He knows the power of sex and he intends to keep us entangled in little sex as opposed to experiencing God-sized, big sex. That's how intentional he is. The Evil One uses our sexuality, yet he never satisfies us sexually, because lust always says, "More, more, more."

I've never met a person who said, "Ed, you know what, lust is great! It's brought us closer together. I've taken a swan dive into the cesspool of lust and it's been great. It's worked wonders for our marriage. The wife and I are closer than ever."

We need to know what the enemy's game is all about so we can see it coming and take precautions. We need to see it clearly because God wants the best for us. He wants us to experience greatness and fullness, and we can when we know what the Evil One is up to and work to avoid the traps.

The enemy doesn't want you to know that the best sex is with your spouse. He wants you to be afraid of true openness and intimacy in marriage. He wants you to think that lust is better than love. But the truth is that lust keeps you looking and hoping for something that's unreal and unattainable rather than focusing on what's real and true, which is intimacy with your spouse. That is an important reason why the Sexperiment has been such a blessing to so many couples; they've been able to get back in touch with what's real in their lives and in their marriage.

There are basically three kinds of lustful personalities. Some people are *recreational lusters*. Lust will kind of hit you every now and then and upset the apple cart of your walk with the Lord. You might see a scene in a movie that feeds a little bit of lust. Then you confess it, turn from it, and get cleaned up. You say, "You know, it's not that big of a problem for me. I've got other issues in my life. I've got other bags and baggage to mess with, you know? This doesn't really mess with me."

Maybe you're an *occupational luster*. You've rented some movies that you would not want anyone to know about. You go places. You've had conversations. You've read novels, magazines, whatever, that you don't really want people to know about and you have sort of a secret lust life, a secret thought life. You dabble in porn online, dabble in immorality, and dabble with the dog bed. And you're on the verge, maybe the edge and the ledge, of falling into the dog bed. You're kind of walking around it.

Then, there's another group who are more like *obsessional lusters*. There's a whole secret side to you that no one knows about. You're spending hundreds, maybe thousands of dollars on pornography and lust and prostitutes and massage parlors and no one knows about your private obsession. You're saying to yourself, "Man, if anybody knew what I was involved in and with and what I was doing, they would just dog me out!"

If you're obsessed with lust, you probably find yourself arranging your life to satisfy its pull. You have these urges, these desires, and you say to yourself time and time again, "I *need* this. Sex is the most important need that I have. I've got to have it."

Masturbation

Pornography and lust fuel masturbation. In most cases, if a person is involved in one, they're involved in the other. What's masturbation? It's having sex with yourself—autoeroticism. It takes no effort to be involved in masturbation. It's the lazy way to get your desires fulfilled. You don't have to work on a relationship. You don't have to risk being intimate. You don't have to be vulnerable. You don't have to communicate. You don't have to engage mentally, physically, or spiritually. There's no operating from the same page. There's no unselfishness. It's just "I will satisfy myself. I'll take sex out of context and have sex with myself."

There's no way to build intimacy and oneness in marriage when one or both spouses is investing energy in satisfying personal physical desires rather than sharing those desires as an intimate moment in the marriage bed.

Pornography, lust, and masturbation are like a never-ending cycle. When you get into one, the others just feed into this behemoth that gradually takes over your life. No matter how much you try to tell yourself it's not hurting anyone, it's not true. It hurts you. It hurts your spouse. It hurts your marriage because the time and attention you would devote to building oneness and intimacy is being invested in activity that can only tear you down rather than build you up.

Infidelity

Infidelity is painful. Whether it's an online affair, a love affair with porn, or an actual, outright extramarital affair, it's devastating to the offended spouse and the marriage itself. Keep reading to understand the hurt that infidelity causes.

Dear Ed:

Our marriage was not perfect, but it was ours and it was all we knew. He was my best friend and I trusted him totally. There were signs. I didn't ignore them, but I became suspicious and very observant. I finally got up the nerve to ask him point-blank, face-to-face, "Are you and your co-worker having an affair?" My husband and best friend of many years looked me right in the eyes and lied.

There were times when I knew he was talking with her on the phone. Many times I would put my hand on the phone receiver by my bed and consider picking it up and listening. Then I'd know for certain; no more speculating. But I couldn't do it, because if it were true it would hurt too much and what would I do?

Finally, my suspicions were replaced with fact. My thoughts and actions spun out of control. I became obsessed with the lies, the details of the affair, and the events that led to it. I kept trying to put all the puzzle pieces together. I was taken over by obsessions. Images of my husband and his lover would flash through my mind day and night. I constantly woke to dreams of him and her in bed together. It would play over and over and over. I stopped feeling positive about myself and about life. It was all negative, jealous, enraged, diminished, bitter, frightened, lonely, ugly, mistrustful, exposed. His deception blinded me from how I saw myself. I started doubting and questioning everything about myself. I thought, "It must be me. I must have caused this affair to happen. I must change myself." I felt the fate of our marriage was in my hands.

This letter is an accurate commentary of the dealings and feelings a spouse has when they discover that they've been cheated on. When you engage in sex outside of marriage, you're taking just one aspect of sex—the physical—and doing it with someone in a physical domain. You tell yourself that's all there is to it, that it didn't mean anything. But it's never just sex, even when it is "just sex."

You can't have sex and think it does not affect your soul and your mind. You can't use God's gift that way and not face consequences. When you take sex out of its context, you're abusing it. You're doing a blasphemous act. You're thumbing your nose at God and you're abusing your mind, your body, and your soul.

In the Bible, 1 Thessalonians 4 says a lot about sex: "God wants you to be holy, so you should keep clear of all sexual sin. Then each of you will control your body and live in holiness and honor—not in lustful passion as the pagans do, in their ignorance of God and his ways."*

Sometimes people read Bible passages like this one and they'll react with, "Oh, all that stuff about sexual purity is so archaic. I mean, how irrelevant is that to today's culture? We live in a sexually liberated culture. If the apostle Paul was living today, he wouldn't know what to do." There's nothing further from the truth.

What Paul taught back then is still very relevant today. When Paul wrote to the Thessalonians, his culture was much more decadent than ours today, if you can believe that. That culture was more wheels-off sexually than our culture is right now.

In the letter to Thessalonica, Paul basically is addressing two different schools of thought. One was the Platonic school of thought. Plato taught that the body is bad and the soul is good. And a lot of people bought into that. There are a lot of Christians today who've bought into this Platonic-type mentality because the church has perpetuated this when it comes to sex. The church has been silent about what God discussed freely.

The other half of the group that Paul was addressing was involved in the mystery religions. Now, the mystery religions were wild, because you would go to temple to worship and have sex with prostitutes and whores while worshipping. They believed this would bless their finances and bless their crops. I'll bet the men were flocking to church!

Rome, in Paul's day, was totally off the chain! Back then, a normal Roman man would have three wives. One would be his "baby mama." Another one would be like his intellectual companion. The third one would be his sex slave.

Homosexuality was rampant in Rome then too. A lot of people in the church of Thessalonica had lived as homosexuals and fornicators. Maybe they were not spiritually strong enough to resist the sex-

---

* 1 Thessalonians 4:3–5, NLT

ual temptations that were so openly flaunted before them. So there was this sexual freewheeling going on when Paul said, "It is God's will that you should be sanctified..."* What does the word *sanctified* mean? It basically means to be set apart. Once we receive Christ, the Holy Spirit comes in and redecorates our lives from the inside out and sets us apart from the world.

Paul then tells them that "you should avoid sexual immorality." Now, this word *immorality* is very interesting. In the Greek, it's pronounced *pornea*. We get the word *pornography* from it. What does *pornea* mean? *Pornea* means premarital sex—fornication, adultery, homosexuality, and a list of other sins. If you want your judgment clouded, if you want to be confused and messed up, just get involved in sexual sin. It engulfs the totality of who we are. So we should distance ourselves from sexual immorality.

"[E]ach of you should learn to control his own body," Paul told them. That means we can learn this. It's a process that happens from the inside out. Our bodies do matter. Our matter matters. It matters to you what you do with your body, and it matters to your spouse.

Unforgiveness

It's devastating to be hurt by the one person you've vowed to have a lifelong connection with under God. Infidelity, secret pornography addictions, Internet affairs, and other breaches of trust wreak havoc on a marriage. These behaviors are wrong, and there's no defense for them. But once they occur, the offended spouse has to make a choice: "Am I going to continue living in anger and resentment and unforgiveness? Or will I, by the grace of God, do my part to get our marriage back on track?" There's no taking the hurt back once it's done, but unforgiveness only makes the situation worse.

Understand that by forgiving someone, it doesn't mean that you condone the offense. It doesn't give the person license to go and do it again. You're not giving them a free pass because, truthfully, if

---

* 1 Thessalonians 4:3

the offending spouse is sincere about wanting to make amends and repair the damage done to the relationship and restore it to wholeness, there's some major work to be done.

"But how can I forget what he did? Let alone forgive?"

No one's asking you to forget, not right now, anyway. But you can begin praying for the heart to forgive. Maybe you'll never forget, and no one's really asking you to, though God forgives and forgets. Our repentant sin is, to Him, as far as the east is from the west.* Maybe you're not ready for your spouse's transgression to be taken that far away in your heart, but the offense has to be removed from the center of your relationship in order to move forward.

Oneness cannot grow in the midst of unforgiveness. You cannot grow in oneness if you won't forgive. Your spouse cannot grow toward oneness if he or she lives under the sphere of being unforgiven.

Not only does your spouse need to experience forgiveness, but so do you. Forgive—for the sake of yourself and the sake of your marriage. It takes a lot of emotional and spiritual energy not to forgive, energy that could better be used to build a solid foundation of trust, intimacy, and ultimately, oneness.

Ephesians 4:32 is a verse that puts the truth right out there: *"Be kind and compassionate to one another, forgiving each other, just as in Christ God forgave you."*

During our wedding ceremony, my father, Dr. Ed Young, challenged Lisa and me with this verse. He told us that if we were to reach the apex in marriage that God had in store for us, we had to live this verse out every day. For thirty years, this has been our life-long marriage verse. And it's all about forgiveness.

Abuse

Maybe you've experienced a lot of hurt in your marriage. Maybe your spouse keeps saying "I'm sorry" and all the apology is to you are

---

* Psalm 103:12

empty words because of continued repetition of hurt and pain. Abusive behavior can take many forms, but most frequently it is physical, mental, emotional, or sexual.*

Oneness can never be built on a foundation of abuse. Nakedness can only happen in an atmosphere of trust, and abuse kills trust in a relationship. Furthermore, an abusive marriage is not stable, and stability is a major component of the kind of intimacy that leads to openness in marriage.

Some Christian wives have submitted to abuse out of a distorted interpretation of Ephesians 5:22–23. But Paul reminds husbands to love their wives as Christ loved the church. "Husbands ought to love their wives as their own bodies. He who loves his wife loves himself. After all, no one ever hated his own body, but he feeds and cares for it, just as Christ does the church."† So if abusive behavior is a part of your marriage, unless you take immediate steps to stop the abuse and learn healthy ways to express anger, frustration, and rage, it will block you and your mate from developing true intimacy.

Some spouses are blocked from being naked and open in marriage because of abuse experienced in the past, either while growing up or maybe even in a previous marriage. The abuse they experienced blocks their ability to trust in marriage. Spouses who were sexually abused during childhood or adolescence often have emotional barriers or walls that hinder them from experiencing the nakedness in marriage that leads to a healthy bond of oneness.

Any kind of abuse is an abuse of trust, and trust is essential to building intimacy and openness. As covenant partners, it is the duty of both spouses to work toward moving past the abuse to get on the road to oneness. No matter who suffered the abuse, it's not just his

---

* We want to be very clear on this issue. If you are in an environment where you are facing physical abuse and endangerment of any kind, get out immediately. Seek the help of law enforcement and close friends. In no way should you remain held in a situation that threatens your health or your life, or the lives of those close to you such as your children.

† Ephesians 5:28–29

problem or her problem. It's a problem for both spouses. It's a problem for the marriage.

Abuse is a monster, a giant, and it can be frightening to confront, whether it occurred in the past or is happening in your marriage right now. But just as God equipped David with the courage and wisdom to confront and defeat the giant Goliath, He will equip you with the tools you need to take down the abuse monster that is (whether you know it or not) keeping up a wall that blocks intimacy between you and your spouse.*

The giant of abuse is not too big to be taken down! If you are sincere about taking your marriage to a deeper level of intimacy, openness, and oneness, pray and ask God to equip you with the weapons you need to fight the giant.

Any of the intimacy blockers that you just read about may need to be considered before entering into the Sexperiment. After all, the entire point is to help you grow closer. You and your spouse may need to determine whether the intimacy blockers can be addressed through the challenge or whether they need to be considered before entering the challenge.

Look in the Mirror

When I look at my marriage with my wife, it reveals my true self. That's why Lisa and I wrote a book called *The Marriage Mirror*. Marriage truly is a mirror because it reflects both spouses as their best and worst selves. As I look into Lisa's eyes, I see a big mirror. When she looks into my eyes, she sees a mirror image of Lisa at her best and Lisa at her worst.

One of the reasons people bolt on marriage is because they don't

---

* 1 Samuel 17

like what they see reflected back. They don't like their junk and their funk being shown back to them. They don't like to be confronted with their inconsistencies, because when you do look at your spouse, you see reflected back *your* best and *your* worst. That's why so many marriages don't have intimacy and so many marriages end up in the deep weeds; people don't like what they see in the mirror. So people go from relationship to relationship and from bed to bed. And when the situation becomes too close or too intimate, they're out of there. They bail.

Other spouses stay in their relationship, but they play hide-and-seek in the bedroom. Now, when I say hide-and-seek in the bedroom, I'm talking about spouses who hide from lovemaking, because when couples make love, we have got to reveal everything.

Intimacy in marriage is essential, so we have to get naked. As I mentioned earlier, in marriage we're emotionally naked, we're financially naked, we're spiritually naked, and we're physically naked. So if we stay away from the bedroom, if we use all of those sexcuses we talked about in chapter two, we will never have the intimacy—being into me, seeing into me—like spouses should.

Spouses play hide-and-seek because they are afraid of or don't like their anger, their resentment. So they check out physically or they tell themselves, "You know what? I don't really dig it, so I'm just not going to have sex that much."

The tragedy in this is that if you don't have sex very much, you don't really have to get to know your spouse. And that's the awesome thing about the Sexperiment. You can run, baby, but you can't hide. In the challenge, you and your spouse will have sex so much that you will have to talk. There's no way around it. You will have to deal with the issues that are blocking intimacy in your marriage.

The Sexperiment puts it all out there—the good, the bad, and the ugly. The closer I get to Lisa, the more I see my good and my bad; the more I see Lisa's good and Lisa's bad.

But truthfully, that's the kind of openness and vulnerability that builds oneness in marriage. The enemy wants you to think that you cannot show any unpleasantness, or that you can't accept any unpleasantness in marriage, but that's not a real marriage. Covenant marriage can survive the negatives, and couples can even use them to build and fortify intimacy and openness in the relationship. Now is the time, as you take on the challenge, to see whether you are able to love past the "dirty fingernails."

We should all strive to be the best person we can, for ourselves and for our spouse. Nevertheless, we have to stay in prayer so that we can look past each other's negatives, as Christ has looked past ours, and by his grace continue on the journey of becoming one. Because of his unconditional love we can be naked before Christ, dirt and all. In marriage we should strive to express unconditional love so we can be naked before each other.

Action Steps

1. Share with your spouse how you believe the Sexperiment can help you grow in openness. Remember, it's all about getting "naked."

2. Rank your personal level of "nakedness" in your marriage. Are you fully naked? If not, consider what may be holding you back, whether it be baggage from your past or present intimacy blockers. This is where the real vulnerability begins.

3. Compliment your spouse on the ways that she/he loves you and allows you to feel loved and accepted, even with dirty fingernails.

4. What behaviors inhibit openness and intimacy in your marriage bed (for example, it could be something ranging from allowing kids to sleep in your bed, sleeping in separate bedrooms, extended periods of time without sexual intercourse, harboring unforgiveness, or even abusive behavior, etc.)?

5. Sit down with your spouse and plan how you will make those behaviors a nonissue during the Sexperiment.

——— *Before You Do* ———

*I*t's really inspiring to see a married couple who have shared their love in openness and honesty. We see it often in elderly couples and it makes us smile. We see it in couples who have been married for twenty or thirty years and we think, "I want that too." Couples planning to marry should go into the union with a heart that is willing to be open, showing all—good, bad, and ugly.

You can lay the foundation now for your future together. Are you hiding major issues from the person you're planning to marry? If you're hiding parts of your personality now, you'll keep doing it in the future. Furthermore, a love that cannot withstand a little dirt under the fingernails certainly cannot withstand the other marital pressures that are sure to come.

Hopefully, you and your future mate are involved in premarital counseling with a qualified Christian counselor. A counseling session is an ideal time to discuss your expectations for marriage, including children, career, finances, sex, dealing with in-laws and extended family, and more.

Being naked in marriage—physically, mentally, and spiritually—takes real effort given in an atmosphere of love and trust. At times it will be challenging, but if you keep Christ at the center of your marriage, you'll get there. Remember the covenantal nature of your marriage.

Talk with your future spouse about why a covenant is different from a contract. Recognize that it is the power of Christ that will hold your marriage together rather than any individual traits and characteristics you possess.

As you plan to spend your lives together, examine yourselves to determine how you may grow closer to Christ.

Discuss with each other how being close to him will help you understand the kind of love and security you will need to empower you to be naked and open in marriage.

The Yoke Is Not a Joke

You can never achieve oneness with a person when you are unequally yoked, so keep your dating relationships targeted to persons who have the potential to become a husband or wife. God insists on spiritual compatibility. That means hanging out only with people who share in God's vision and design for sexual intercourse. He expects you to date those people.

Now, you're not going to have as many dates. But it's not about quantity; it's about quality. The dates you have will be great because one of the few you date has the potential to become your mate in marriage.

Getting married is serious in the eyes of God, so it should be serious to you, too. God tells us to reserve sex for the marriage bed, but let's leave that out of it for the moment. You also need to abstain from premarital sex to keep your head and your emotions clear regarding who you plan to marry and why. Abstaining keeps you from marrying someone because you think the sex is good and that it will keep you wanting to be together.

Premarital sex abuses and it confuses. It abuses your mind, your body, and your soul. It abuses the other person, even though he or she may be a willing participant. You strip that person of humanity while you're stripping yourself of your humanity.

You can't just say, "You're just genitals, and I'm just genitals. Let's just use each other's genitals and everything will be cool in the little bed."

No! You're taking something away from God and from yourself. You're taking something special out of its context and saying, "It's just physical." But it's not just physical. It's about full and complete openness and oneness in marriage. At the same time, it's about the Trinity in you. So don't get that kind of naked until your wedding night!

5

Looking Out for Number One

*O*ne of the greatest lessons we can learn in marriage is about the benefits that come from spouses putting each other first. That's what it means to look out for number one. Your marriage is your number-one relationship on earth.

In too many marriages, looking out for number one means each spouse looking out for the self. That's not a true picture of marriage, though. Marriage is more about giving than receiving. Looking out for number one should mean each spouse giving 100 percent to the marriage, not each giving 50 percent. When both give 100 percent, the needs of both spouses will be met.

Looking out for number one is something married couples get better at, I think, the longer we stay together. Putting Lisa's needs first is something that I've learned over the years. She wants to share a story with you about what it means to look out for number one. This is one of those times when I really got it right as a husband.

Lisa's Story

I want to tell you about the greatest gift that Ed has ever given me, but to do that I have to give you some background. Ed and I have been married for nearly thirty years and we have four children. When I found out I was pregnant with Laurie and Landra (our twins), we moved quickly from a family of four to a family of six.

A couple of months before we brought the twins home from the hospital, I went to the mailbox and pulled out a *Focus on the Family* magazine. That issue featured an article on the needs of men. It said that one of the greatest needs of a man was a tranquil home, and I thought, "Oh, Lord, please no. If this is the truth, we are doomed."

I thought, "Poor Ed is never going to get his needs met, because I just can't envision tranquility in our home." After the twins were born, Ed was much better than I was at airing his frustrations. He would say things like, "Will we ever be able to go out to eat again?" "How are we going to make it?" "What are we going to do?"

Meanwhile, I was always trying to keep that tranquil feeling alive by saying things like, "Oh, it's going to be fine." But inside I was telling myself, "It's not going to be fine." After about six months of this, my frustration had mounted because I had kept my true feelings bottled up inside. I wasn't honest with Ed. Instead I took out my frustration on little things that he would do. I would pick and snap at him and the children.

Eventually, Ed, in wisdom, asked, "Lisa, what's the deal?"

And finally I shared my frustrations with him. "You talk about how hard it is and ask what are we going to do, but you leave every morning and you look good when you go out that door and you go to work and you eat lunch with grown-ups. You come and go as you please, pretty much. And I feel trapped, like I am caught here in this perpetual maze of life in our home. And then there are those trips that you take sometimes; you know, maybe once a year you go off with a couple of guys and go fishing, and I don't get to do that."

What an unbelievably refreshing feeling it was to actually share my feelings and to have Ed listen with compassion and caring. This is when Ed gave me the best and most fitting gift I had ever received. He told me, "Lisa, I tell you what I am going to do. You are going to go on a trip." The gift that he gave me was that I got to choose where

I wanted to go and who I wanted to go with. He suggested a spa trip with some girlfriends, but I opted instead for a B and B in Jefferson, Texas, completely alone.

It was so important to me to get away. The journal I brought with me had about 300 blank pages, but I filled two pages while I was away those two nights. I never had time to do that at home. I so appreciated having time alone to meditate, to thank God, to pray, and to spend some time alone with God. For me, the greatest part was just being alone and resting, refocusing and realizing the goals God had for my life.

I took time to evaluate my spiritual pilgrimage, my pilgrimage as a wife, as a homemaker, and with the children. I set some goals for myself, for our family, for my relationship with Ed and things that we would want to do with our children. And then I strategized how to meet those goals. It is no good to set goals if you don't strategize how it's going to be done.

But after that I took time for pampering. I slept. I didn't fix anybody's meals. I didn't take anyone to the restroom. I didn't cut any meat for anyone. I didn't wipe anyone's nose. I just took care of me. And I loved it. I was totally by myself and it was great. But the best thing I did while I was there was that I wrote down a list of our family members and thought of ways that they had blessed me. I wrote positive characteristics that I love about our children. No critical things, just positive things.

And then when I got home, I was able to say thank you to each of them and tell them, "This is what I appreciate about you." I saved the best for last, and I wrote a list about Ed. I thought about the days of our courtship, special things that we did, little pet names that we had for each other. I took time to reminisce about things in the present that are great: his creativity, his laughter, how proud I am of the job that he does at the church.

That trip was very important to me, and probably a lot of that is due to the fact that Ed sacrificed for me to go. It wasn't easy for him. He rearranged his schedule. He had to take some time off. It was a sacrifice for him, but he was willing to do it. Not for a fishing trip, not for anything else, but for me. And that meant the world to me.

Tune in to Your Spouse

In the days before digital features and scan buttons on radios, you had to "tune in" with a dial to find the station you wanted. Sometimes you could find the station right away because there was a strong, clear signal. At other times, you would have to toggle the knob back and forth, trying to hit just the right spot to tune in to the channel you wanted.

Marriage can be a lot like trying to tune in to those old radios. We tune in to our spouses, hoping to lock onto the right signal. Sometimes the signals are strong, and at other times they are weak. Like when Lisa was struggling with trying to keep a tranquil home after the birth of our twin girls. The signal she gave off at first was weak. But then, as I was able to tune in to her needs, I hit a signal that came through loud and clear. She needed some "me" time.

The tuning-in process is an important part of sexual intimacy in marriage, also. Since men and women are wired different sexually, there's some tuning in that has to happen.

Learning how to tune in is a great benefit of the Sexperiment challenge. By making sex a priority in your relationship for one week, you and your spouse will begin to tune in to each other's needs.

When the husband is thinking about her needs and the wife is thinking about his needs, you'll have two people tuning in to the pace of their collective passion. If you want to get your partner in the mood, you'll have to approach him or her the way he or she wants to be approached.

Some couples are clueless about how male and female sex drives are different, and this can cause lot of tension in the bedroom. I've always believed that when it comes to sex, men are sprinters and women are long-distance runners.

In an instant, a man can be ready to sprint into sex. It doesn't matter if he's just had a major argument with his wife or if his bank account is overdrawn. He transitions quickly. A woman more or less jogs into sex. A husband experiences sex, and from his sexual experiences flow his feelings. The wife is the polar opposite. She has to experience feelings before she can experience physical intimacy.

The trouble comes when the husband expects his wife to sprint and the wife expects her husband to jog along into sex. He is aggressive and takes initiative as he sprints into lovemaking. Meanwhile, she meanders along, winding her way into the mood.

In order for sexual intimacy to be mutually enjoyable, both spouses have to tune in to the other's needs and wants. Marriage God-style is all about the other. You submit your desires and needs to the other.

Sex Is About the "Yes"

Not long after I began preaching about the Sexperiment, Lisa and I attended a football game. A couple in their seventies was sitting behind us, and during the middle of the game the man leaned down and said, "Hey, thank you for talking so openly about sex." I looked at Lisa, who was sitting next to a friend, and we had to chuckle at this exchange.

At that point I said, "Well, I appreciate it. And you're welcome."

Then he added, "My wife has always been available for me sexually. She has pretty much always said yes."

That was a little too much information, but we got his point. Sex is about the yes. I know it's not possible for both spouses to be available for sex at all times. So sex is about the yes, but we have to know our noes to understand when to say yes.

Sex, or the absence of it, so often is the elephant in the room that we don't want to talk about but everyone is thinking about.

After marriage, so many spouses do a pushback rather than a

lean-toward. They're so busy trying to maintain their individuality that they toss the needs of their spouse aside. They say, "This is my body. I have my rights." But that's not what God says. Once we get married, we give up our rights and we steward our spouse's body. Marriage is both what you don't do and what you do before you say "I do."

The Bible gives us a great picture of what sexual intercourse in marriage should be: "Drink water from your own cistern, running water from your own well. Should your springs overflow in the streets, your streams of water in the public squares? Let them be yours alone, never to be shared with strangers. May your fountain be blessed, and may you rejoice in the wife of your youth. A loving doe, a graceful deer—may her breasts satisfy you always, may you ever be captivated by her love. Why be captivated, my son, by an adulteress? Why embrace the bosom of another man's wife? For a man's ways are in full view of the Lord, and He examines all his paths. The evil deeds of a wicked man ensnare him; the cords of his sin hold him fast. He will die for lack of discipline, led astray by his own great folly."*

Learning how to be supportive and accommodating is of major importance in marriage because, basically, we're selfish creatures. It's not in our nature to always put the needs of our spouse before our own, but it's critical to the success of a marriage.

The Sexperiment, as well as ongoing sexual fulfillment in marriage, requires putting your needs aside to consider those of your spouse. A week of sex requires accommodating the marriage and accommodating your spouse, even if it's inconvenient for you.

That's why a strong MWE (marital work ethic) is important. Marriage is spelled W-O-R-K. If we're going to open the door to marital fulfillment, we have to maintain a tireless marital work ethic.

We work to get to the point of marriage. Dating, communicating, and learning about each other take work. It's fun, but it's work. We put a lot into it.

---

* Proverbs 5:15–21

The trouble happens when, once we're married, a lot of us stop working. We end up working at other relationships or other things. We'll work on our relationship with our kids. We'll work on a relationship at the office or on climbing the corporate ladder. We'll work on our golf game or work at playing tennis or at decorating a house. So often, though, we neglect working on the foundation of the marriage.

Can you honestly say that you put as much effort into pleasing your spouse as you do into pleasing your boss at work? Do you work as hard to please your spouse as you do to please your kids?

What if you took the same energy and effort you put into your job or your hobbies and put it into your marriage? What would happen if you treated your office or work site like you treat your home? You can't just show up in a career and put in a mediocre effort. If you do, you won't last long.

We have to work at having a good relationship in marriage. It takes work to learn how to prioritize date night over softball night. It takes work to carve out quality time and communicate to learn each other's needs. It takes work to put the marriage before our other family members, friends, job, or even church members.

Looking out for number one means that husbands need to work on creativity in marriage, through meaningful conversation and romance. Wives need to work on creativity in sex and understanding the importance of the physical aspect to their husbands.

Marriage is not complex, despite what our culture espouses. Just go to any local bookstore to the section on marriage and relationships. Those shelves are loaded with all the books on marriage and the intricacies of relationships. And listening to people on talk shows and all the relational experts only makes it more confusing. None of that builds a marriage. It's really about work.

Use the Sexperiment to begin the work in your marriage that you may have neglected until now. During your week of sex, look at your spouse with different eyes. Look at her heart. Look at his needs. As you look beyond yourself to the needs of your spouse, hopefully you will reconnect to the qualities of the person you fell in love with and decided to marry. When people claim to have become bored with their spouse, it's usually because one or both spouses have failed to put in the work.

People love the feeling of ecstasy that comes from romance and sexual excitement. The problem is we've been conditioned to believe that experiencing such thrills is only possible by having multiple sexual partners or conquests.

I'll be the first to admit that marriage is not ecstasy, excitement, and romance every second of every day. But I'll also tell you that it's possible to have these experiences continually within the context of a monogamous marital union. Monogamy does not mean monotony! So Lisa and I are encouraging spouses to put forth the energy and effort that so often go into extramarital affairs into having a love affair with your own spouse.

How to Have an Affair with Your Spouse

Yes, you read that last sentence correctly. Have a love affair with your spouse! People invest amazing amounts of time and energy to have extramarital affairs. Why not use that energy instead to have an affair with your own spouse? With the effort of a few simple steps, you will find in your own spouse what you might have thought could only be found outside the marriage.

Believe That It Can Happen to You

Every human being has the potential to get entangled in an extramarital affair. I don't care who you are. It *can* happen to you.

King David in the Bible is described as "a man after God's own heart," yet even he fell to the temptation of lust and adultery.* The Bible also says that "when you are tempted," God will provide a

* Acts 13:22

means of escape. So God doesn't say *if* you are tempted, but *when*. We're going to be tempted.

As a single young man, I was naïve in thinking that I would never be attracted to another woman after Lisa and I married. We were on our honeymoon at the Mana Kai Hotel in Hawaii, sitting by the pool, and I saw this beautiful woman walk by. Oh, man! That was my first reality check that marriage doesn't kill our attraction for someone other than our spouse.

The first look is not the sin. The sin is what you do after that look. When it becomes attraction that segues into an ungodly action and you paint pictures in your mind and begin to lust after that person—that's where it goes south.

Cultivate Your Relationship with Your Spouse

Get into your spouse. Don't spend your energy cultivating a relationship with a third party. When it comes down to it, put the most energy into your marriage. Because a great marriage doesn't just happen. It takes work.

My marriage to Lisa doesn't just happen. It has not been an effortless journey. The level of intimacy in our marriage is not a natural thing, because I am a self-centered person. I say things I shouldn't say. I think things I shouldn't think. I do things I shouldn't do. So does Lisa.

For three decades we have worked at our marriage. Many times we don't feel like working on our marriage, but we do. We're very, very intentional about it. We've gone through dry seasons. We've gone through seasons when we were on a roll. But I can tell you with complete confidence that Lisa and I have a stronger love today than we did when we first met at age fifteen, because of our marital work ethic.

Whenever you see or feel your marriage drifting away from the goal of looking out for number one—and it will happen—you've got to be the one to step up and step out to take the initiative and ride the crest of creativity. Because if you are not careful, your marriage can be lulled into a state of predictability, which leads to boredom and an ultimate search for excitement elsewhere.

When you were dating your spouse, you likely pursued each other with creativity, excitement, and passion. Keep it going! Use the Sexperiment as your starting point. Never stop dating your spouse, and you won't hit the wall of monotony and predictability. Cultivate your relationship with your mate.

Borrow Pain from the Future

When you see someone you're attracted to (because it will happen), here's something that I challenge you to do. I do this. Borrow pain from the future.

What do I mean by that? You borrow pain from the future when you encounter someone at the health club or the grocery store and think, "OK, what happens if I hook up with this person who I see at the health club or wherever? We're connecting and all this, but if I take this to the next level, what is going to happen? Man, I'm going to sign up for some serious pain."

Did you ever watch professional wrestling? Do you remember Ric "Nature Boy" Flair? How about Dusty Rhodes, aka "The American Dream"? Dusty Rhodes used to say this all the time: "There's gonna be some serious pain tonight in the house!"

If you're considering giving in to an extramarital affair, think about the serious pain of adultery. Think about coming before God, sitting down with your spouse, and telling him or her what you've done. Think about sitting down with your kids and telling them. Your co-workers, family members, or church members. It's not worth it. It's just not worth it. The quick thrill is not worth the long-term collateral damage of adultery.

Affairs don't just happen in a flash. They happen when we ignore temptation's warning signs and move ahead into the danger zone.

We all have to convince ourselves it can happen. That includes me, and Lisa, too. If you're tiptoeing around the fringe of adultery, stop the connection while it's still in its early stages. Don't walk by his office. Don't run around the neighborhood when you know she might be outside watering her flowers. Don't go to the gym when you know that person is going to be there.

The Bible tells us to flee from sexual immorality. What does the word *flee* mean? It means get the heck outta there; that's what it means! You've just got to get away from adultery while you still can.

Realize the Reality

Let's say someone at work has caught your eye. You see this person always putting his or her best foot forward, always well dressed, always smiling, always polite, always has nice breath, white teeth, whatever.

Well, that person is not your spouse, so you're not seeing the person's unattractive side. We see the real deal in our spouse and our marriage—mortgage payments, car repairs, kids, homework, and all that stuff. So it's just fantasy versus reality.

And this is what's so sinister about adultery. All the people I know in my life who have committed adultery eventually end up facing the same junk that they didn't deal with in their marriage. They spend all this money, time, energy, creativity, and innovation with another person when they could have just stopped and watered their own grass.

The Bible says, "Take captive every thought to make it obedient to Christ."* Every thought. You're in Hawaii with your new bride and you see the girl? Whoa! I've got to take that thought captive. Or you've been married for fifteen years and you meet this hot guy at the gym. Delete! Delete!

Delete every adulterous thought before it takes hold of you. Ask yourself, "Does this thought honor God or not?" If it doesn't, throw it out! Delete! Delete! Delete!

---

* 2 Corinthians 10:5

Connect with Your Spouse Regularly

The intentional effort of connecting with your spouse regularly has to do with conversation. It has to do with emotional connection. It has to do with physical connection.

Spouses are supposed to connect regularly. We're to serve each other in all the ways that we could ever think of. The marriage relationship is compared to Christ's relationship to the church. That's our standard. That's how holy, that's how pure, that's how awesome the connection is.

A powerful way to connect with your spouse is by making your spouse your hero. He or she is the person you look up to. The person you cheer for. The person you admire.

If you have a spouse who loves you and who has stuck with you through the good and the bad, the hard times and the great times, the poor times and the rich times, then that's your hero. A spouse like that deserves praise greater than what any sports star or public figure has ever gotten.

Are you giving your spouse his or her due? Are you praising your spouse in public? When was the last time you went to dinner with a group of people and you just made sure that sometime during the dinner you brought up something publicly that your spouse did for you? "Guys, I have to tell you what my wife did for me..."

Wives, brag about your husbands. Men love to see our names up in lights. We love to hear our name in public. Just think how incredible it would be if we would remember to praise our spouses publicly.

Be each other's number-one fan. *That's* looking out for number one, and that's what makes the marriage a great relationship that can sustain closeness and intimacy, no matter what. We've already discussed that marriage is not just one continuous string of excitement and ecstasy. It's so much deeper than that. And by respecting your marriage as the number-one relationship you have on earth, you will experience the fullness and true intimacy of the covenantal bond God designed as a gift to us.

Action Steps

1. Make a case for your spouse to be your hero. Write down the characteristics that you most admire about your spouse and the things you would want other people to know about him or her.

2. Get together with your spouse and determine seven ways that you will make a deliberate effort to tune in to each other mentally, emotionally, and physically during the Sexperiment.

3. How can you initiate a love affair with your spouse during the Sexperiment? Think about the things you would do if you were trying to pursue your spouse in a relationship today. What would get your spouse's attention? What would turn your spouse on? What would turn your spouse off? Pay attention to your spouse's needs, wants, likes, and dislikes and make your marriage a true love affair during the Sexperiment. Use what you learn during the Sexperiment to maintain creativity and intimacy as an ongoing component of your marriage.

4. Make a list of what you believe your spouse's needs are. Ask your spouse to do the same. Review each other's lists so you can determine whether you are on target in being in tune with each other's needs.

5. Discuss with your spouse what it means for the two of you to look out for number one, which is your marriage. How does that understanding look and function in your marriage?

—— *Before You Do* ——

When you enter into covenant marriage, you are letting go of self. Of course, you both will still be individuals. But as spouses, you have the added responsibility of "tuning in" to the needs of someone else.

The time to start that process is now. Pay attention and don't assume. A lot of people are guilty of assuming what their spouse wants or needs, but their perceptions may be far from reality. When you learn to put the marriage above your individual wants and needs, you learn one of the most critical components to marital harmony and longevity.

Now is your time to learn each other, to tune in to each other. The romance part is wonderful and adds the extra spice needed to keep the relationship alive and fresh. But the best romance comes when both are tuned in to each other's needs, wants, and desires.

If you know anything about gardening or lawn care, you know what happens when you neglect or ignore your lawn or your garden, even for a little while. Weeds start to grow, and even take over. The grass gets high. Soon it's not very pretty and you feel overwhelmed by the responsibility and the effort required to get things back on track.

A lot of people get into that kind of rut in marriage. They neglect their spouse's needs and never develop a marital work ethic. By the time they take a good look at their marriage, it's neglected and overtaken by deep weeds.

Your time of engagement is your time of preparation, a time of learning how to merge your life with another person's—for life. I talk a lot about having a strong marital work ethic. You can develop a strong premarital work ethic, which will help you lay the foundation for tuning in and building a strong MWE.

——— *The Yoke Is Not a Joke* ———

*B*eing single means having the prerogative to concern yourself with your own needs and wants. Sure, you care about friends, family members, and neighbors, but you don't really have to concern yourself with putting their needs before your own. Not most of the time, anyway.

If you've never been married, you cannot understand what it means to put a relationship or another person first. But to help you understand, talk to a couple you know, respect, and admire because of the quality of their marriage. Ask them to share with you how they have journeyed together, learning how to look out for number one.

Ask them to share, if they can, some of the challenges they encountered in learning to look out for number one. Also ask them to tell you the rewards of long-term partnership in marriage.

Think about what they have shared with you and honestly ask yourself if you are ready for the kind of commitment marriage requires. Think about the qualities and personality traits you desire in a mate and how those traits will help you look out for the needs of your spouse and look out for number one. Furthermore, make a list of your own wants and needs so that you can know the kind of person you need to be attentive to your wants and needs.

Please don't make the mistake of spending so much time worrying about how you can attract someone that you neglect knowing the kind of person you are attracted to. You are worth having someone meet your needs and wants.

Dating is the time for you to get to know the kind of person who will be concerned about meeting your needs and whose needs you will want to meet as well.

6

Leaving Lust Vegas

*I*n my book *Fatal Distractions,* I told the story of a snake that my father captured when I was a boy. My dad put the snake in a jar and left it behind the house. He wasn't sure if the snake was poisonous, but he warned me, "Ed, don't touch the snake. You understand me?" Then he walked inside.

What do you think I did? I looked at that snake and said, "Man, this snake's not poisonous. I've watched all the outdoor shows." So I unscrewed the top of the jar. Meanwhile, all my neighborhood friends were trying to keep me out of trouble. "Ed, don't do it! Don't do it!"

I told them, "Man, chill! I got this!" Well, I reached my hand in there and picked up the snake. Immediately, I was the man. Everybody was going, "Wow, look at Ed! He's a snake handler. This guy is incredible!"

I was going, "Yeah, you know, you've just got to know your snakes." Without warning, the snake just cranked down on my left index finger. I tried to shake him off, but he wouldn't let go. I got scared and began to scream and cry.

All I can say is, thank God the snake was nonpoisonous. Even though I had been warned, I put myself in danger. I tried to get up close and personal with something that was bound to strike back at me.

Sometimes things that seem harmless can strike back at us in devastating ways. Like lust. Having sexual or romantic thoughts about someone other than your spouse may seem harmless because it's all in your head, or so you think. But lust is like that snake—you can get all up close and personal with it for a while, but eventually, and usually without warning, it will bite. But unlike the snake that bit me as a boy, lust is a venomous creature that can impose horrendous damage on a marriage. When you try to make a pet out of lust, it will bite you!

Maybe it won't seem like it at first, but lust can drain you of the time and energy you need to get closer to your spouse. The Sexperiment—and beyond that, an intimate, meaningful sex life within marriage—requires a commitment of time and energy. Lust will eat away at your resolve to engage in a week of sex with your spouse. It will chip away at your motivation to achieve lasting intimacy in marriage through the Sexperiment.

Some spouses who claim to be too tired or uninterested in sex can still muster the energy to lust after someone they see on television, online, or in the mall. If lust is attacking your marriage and eating away at marital intimacy in your home, there's only one thing to do. You have to get out of "Lust Vegas."

People love the real Las Vegas. Something like thirty million people visit every year. It's a popular place. Almost one thousand flights converge on Sin City every day. Folks go there for lots of different reasons—conventions, destination weddings, shows and attractions . . . But Vegas is really known for gambling.

I read someplace that 87 percent of the people who visit Las Vegas gamble while they're there. Is that surprising to you? Some of those gamblers are high rollers, but many of them are the little old ladies who just love those "one-armed bandits" and cheap buffets.

Whether you're gambling in Las Vegas or someplace else in your life, you risk something. You are trying to beat the odds, and sometimes you do. But ultimately the house wins.

Far too many spouses are gambling with their marriages and

families. Right now, they may be beating the odds. But sooner or later, they're going to have to pay the house. *Because the house always wins.*

Conventional wisdom says you should never gamble more than you can afford to lose. Are you hanging out in Lust Vegas, gambling with a marriage you cannot afford to lose? Can you afford to lose your spouse? Your family? Think about that, because if you're gambling with lust, sooner or later the house—which is the enemy's domain—is going to win. Your house is going to lose.

A lot of people like to hang out in Lust Vegas. They enjoy taking physical, mental, or emotional trips into lust. When they go there, they are rolling the dice, playing the odds, and trying to beat the house with their sexuality.

Maybe you're stuck in Lust Vegas and you want out. It might have been fun at first, but now you're on a losing streak because the house is winning every round! Maybe you've been to Lust Vegas and know that it's not nearly as exciting as the enemy wants you to believe. Now you want to stay out. Maybe you've never been to Lust Vegas and you want to make sure that you never go.

Wherever you are, Lisa and I are excited about your interest in the Sexperiment so you can take or keep your marriage off the gaming table. If you're hanging out in Lust Vegas, the Sexperiment could be the first step to helping you leave and get your marriage to the place God intended it to be.

What's Lust Got to Do with It?

A guy may ask, "What's wrong with thinking about another woman as long as I only have intercourse with my wife?" Or a woman may ask, "What's wrong with a little fantasy, as long as I don't act on it?" Lust circumvents the process of working toward intimacy in marriage. You may think you're doing nothing wrong, because your husband doesn't know that while you're making love you're really thinking about that hot guy who works at the gym. But *you* know.

You can't give 100 percent to establishing and maintaining intimacy with your spouse if there are three people in your marriage bed.

What's lust really got to do with it? A lot. Jesus said that if you even look at someone with lust in your heart, you're committing adultery.* Why? Because emerging out of the heart are evil thoughts, murder, adultery, sexual immorality, theft, false testimony, and slander.† It starts in the heart.

Jesus was saying you have to get out of Lust Vegas because it all starts with the heart. The quality of your marriage greatly depends on whether you're focused on your spouse or fantasizing about being with someone else. That's why it's important to get out of Lust Vegas before you go into the Sexperiment. This is a time of being totally into your spouse. This is the time when you must let go of anyone else who is consuming your interest or attention.

Maybe you are captured by a seductive thought life. Are you risking your marriage with an emotionally adulterous relationship? Adultery isn't just limited to the physical act of sex with someone other than your spouse. Adultery can be emotional or mental as well.

Maybe you are imprisoned by pornography. It's easy these days. Opportunities to nurture lustful thoughts are all around. It's as close as your home computer and as convenient as your mobile phone. And it's free to look, because the porn sites are counting on "the comeback"—a sales strategy similar to how a drug dealer operates.

A drug dealer will give you your first high for free. Maybe even your second one. By the third time, you're looking for him. He knows you're hooked by then, and *that's* when you have to pay. Same thing with porn sites. They give you lots of visual highs for free. And as you get into looking at perfect, airbrushed bodies in all kinds of acrobatic poses and positions, you want more. And that's when you have to pay. But money is just part of the cost involved. In fact, it's probably the smallest price you'll have to pay. The real price you pay,

---

* See Matthew 5:28
† See Matthew 15:19

the heavy price, is in the quality of your marriage and your family relationships.

Opportunities to go to Lust Vegas are cheap and plentiful in our society, so you have to know how to deal with the temptations so you can stay out of there. That's why I'm telling you up front that it won't do any good to participate in the Sexperiment if you're hanging out in Lust Vegas.

If you're there, I want to help you get out. When you leave, you have to go somewhere. And God wants you to reach a dynamic destination. It's all about leaving, but it's also all about going to a new place. That's what this book and this challenge are all about. We want you to discover a place of passion and purpose with your spouse! Because that is the greatest place you can be as a married couple—with each other and away from Lust Vegas.

If you're not in Lust Vegas, I want to help you stay away. I want to tell you about a guy who knew what to do when someone tried to pull him into Lust Vegas. He knew how to keep lustful feelings in check. This guy, when invited to enter the city gates, simply chose to walk away. He left Lust Vegas. If you haven't left already, hopefully, after reading his story you will get out of there and stay out.

Putting Lust in Check

The guy I want you to know, understand, and get up close and personal with is Joseph. No, not adoptive father of Jesus. This Joseph, whose story begins in Genesis 39, is a truly amazing dude.

Let me give you the *Wikipedia* version of his life. Joseph grew up in a dysfunctional family. His family put the "diss" in dysfunctional. I love that the Bible keeps it real! Joseph's dad had multiple wives and concubines and clearly loved one wife more than the others. He had no problem showing favoritism among his sons, either. There was incest, jealousy, and strife in the family among the wives, between the brothers—everywhere.

Joseph's father, Jacob, had gone out of his way to show everybody that Joseph was his favorite child. He was the golden boy who was too good to perform the common labor that his brothers had to do every day. To show how special Joseph was, his dad bought him a Prada coat, just to show everybody that he was the man. (OK, it wasn't really Prada, but it certainly stood out from anything else people were wearing then!)

This coat broadcasted the fact that Joseph was his father's favorite. His brothers were terribly jealous of him. Can you blame them? When they decided they'd had enough of the Dysfunctional Family Feud, the brothers took Joe's coat and smeared some blood on it. Then they ran to their father and said, "Dad, it's terrible! A wild animal ate Joseph alive!"

They were lying, of course. They had actually thrown Joseph into a pit and were going to leave him to die. They reconsidered and chose instead to sell him to an Ishmaelite caravan traveling through on the way to Egypt. The Ishmaelites took Joseph and sold him on an Egyptian trading block.

The Egypt that Joseph was sold into was a culture of contrasts. People were either dirt poor or rolling in serious "coin." Potiphar was one of the Egyptians who was rolling. He was head of the Egyptian CIA and FBI—in other words, a heavy hitter. Potiphar saw Joseph— young, strong, intelligent-looking—and bought him.

Just for a second, put yourself in Joseph's sandals. He had quickly gone from favorite son to anonymous slave. He was a kid who had grown up in a wacked-out household, but he loved the Lord. His leadership skills had been developed there in his family compound, which despite being dysfunctional, had taught him how to run a successful business operation.

Joseph's enslavement thrust him into a perverted culture of sexual immorality, including wife-swapping. Not the kind of swapping we see on those reality TV shows where the wives switch households for a couple of weeks. These dudes were swapping sex partners. Immorality was cool to them because everybody in Egypt was doing it.

While Joseph was checking out his new surroundings, Potiphar's wife started checking him out. Talk about eye candy! This woman was a real babe; let's call her "Hotiphar." We're talking Miss Egypt 500 BC. And she was parading around Joseph in sexy, skimpy outfits. Her husband had brought this young Jewish guy home, and she was determined to sleep with him! That is the mind-set Joseph was dealing with.

And that's what a lot of married people are dealing with today. They're struggling with living in marital purity in the midst of a culture that says do whatever, whenever, and however with whomever you feel like doing it. There are many opportunities for people to do just that. Amazingly, there are even dating websites just for married people who want to have affairs.

In our electronic age, large numbers of married people are having porn affairs. A few clicks of the mouse open up an endless display of scantily clad beauties who seem to want nothing more than to fulfill all your sexual desires. Those women are never tired from working, carpooling, cooking, doing dishes, or taking care of the kids. They always look hot and ready for sex. A man can have one of those women in his mind as often as he wants. No work required. No communication, either. No context. No strings attached. Just an endless sea of beauty to fantasize about. As a husband contemplates sex with these women, the very real and alive spouse he sleeps with starts looking less and less appealing.

Let's go back to our boy Joseph.

New Levels, New Devils

The Lord opened doors for Joseph, even though he was a slave. Potiphar knew that the Lord was with Joseph.* How could he tell? Joseph didn't carry a big scroll of Scripture all the time. He didn't have to

---

* See Genesis 39:3–4

walk around saying, "Hey, I'm a follower of the Lord and if you don't turn, you'll burn." No, Potiphar saw that the Lord had given Joseph success in everything he did.

Potiphar was impressed by what he saw in this smart and anointed young man and made Joseph his personal attendant. He entrusted everything he owned to Joseph's care. Even though technically he was still a slave, Joseph was the man.

Joseph's story holds another profound key principle, aside from being a good example of how to deal with lust, as we shall see later: The greater the blessing, the greater the temptation. The greater the favor of God and the closer you are walking in God's plan, the greater the enemy will ratchet up the temptation stakes. In short: When you reach new levels, you'll face new devils.

A friend of mine told me a while back, "Ed, when people are climbing upward—when they are climbing up the corporate ladder, when they are trying to build the client base, when they're trying to start the company, trying to start the church—rarely do they fall into sexual sin. People fall into sexual sin when they get on top of the ladder."

You've climbed a ladder before, haven't you? When you are climbing, falling down is no problem because you're concentrating on navigating your way to the top. Once you get there, though, there's not as much support and you can easily fall.

We need to be very careful when climbing ladders. It's been said that money and power are the ultimate aphrodisiacs, so when God blesses you with promotion—more authority, more money, more influence—more people are going to see you, and a lot of them are going to make themselves attractive to you to get your attention. These will be people who don't come with the burden of marital problems. They will make it convenient and easy for you to sleep in the wrong bed. So you have to be on guard, because lust can strike at any time, day or night.

No one is immune from lust. Joseph wasn't. You're not. I'm not either. One night Lisa and I shared a meal with some friends at a Dallas restaurant. When we were getting ready to leave, Lisa and these friends went outside to pick up the car while I stopped by the men's room. When I came out, I had to walk by the bar area, which was closed. Just as I was about to go out of the restaurant, the door swung open and standing before me was one of the most beautiful, seductive women I have ever seen in my life. I was attracted to her. Looking at her, I thought, "Unbelievable!"

Now, let me stop here and tell you it is not wrong to be attracted to the opposite sex. We are going to be attracted to members of the opposite sex. Attraction and lust are not the same thing. Lust is attraction taken to a different level. Lust comes into play when an attraction segues into an illicit sexual action that is mental, visual, emotional, or physical. Lust is a God-given desire (the desire for sex) gone haywire!

But as I walked through the empty bar of that restaurant, I was faced with the moment of truth. There was no one around me to say, "Oh, there's Ed Young, pastor of Fellowship Church." Since no one was watching me, I had a choice. I could turn and watch her and go, "Whoa," and follow the path of lust. Or I could keep walking, press the Delete button, and go about my day.

What did I do? I pressed the Delete button. I kept myself on a path of purity. I don't score a 100 every time, but by God's grace and power I've learned to press the Delete button.

Joseph knew how to press the Delete button too. But his problem wasn't him looking at a woman. What got him in trouble was a woman looking at him. Genesis 39:6 says that Joseph was well built and handsome. In the Hebrew language, it means he was "ripped, shredded," and his master's wife took notice.

Having this buff young guy around all the time was getting to be too much for Potiphar's wife, Hotiphar. She was bored with her marriage because all Potiphar had on his mind was work. She said to Joseph, with no great subtlety, "Come to bed with me." She lost it and wanted to turn her natural attraction to the opposite sex into adultery.

Is Your Marriage Full of Lustration?

Focusing your attention beyond a basic attraction to how someone else looks, how someone else dresses, how someone else smells causes mayhem; it causes marital "lustration."

"I wish my husband paid as much attention to his personal grooming as Joe."

"Man, I wish my wife could look like that!"

Looking at someone else with desire eventually leads to comparisons and dissatisfaction. It leads to lustration—the lust causes frustration that your spouse is not like the person you're fantasizing about. The truth is that even the person you're fantasizing about isn't really like that. After they leave the bright lights of the camera that sells you slick fantasies, they go home to lead normal lives—they take out the trash, they wash dishes, they argue with family members, they pick up the kids from day care.

A husband who is fantasizing about that hot babe he saw online is not really making love to his wife when they're having sex. Conversely, a wife won't feel motivated to be intimate with her husband if she's thinking about the guy who compliments her every day. He notices when she wears something new to work. He even notices when she's wearing a different perfume.

Hotiphar was suffering from marital lustration, but Joseph wouldn't go there with her. "With me in charge," he told her, "my master does not concern himself with anything in the house; everything he owns he has entrusted to my care."* Joseph understood the concept of management. He didn't need the seventh commandment

---

* Genesis 39:8

("Do not commit adultery") to know that sleeping with his boss's wife was just plain out of order.

What Happens in Lust Vegas (Never) Stays in Lust Vegas

If you hang around Lust Vegas long enough, sooner or later the lustful feelings will lead to action. Remember, Jesus said it starts with the heart.

The reality is that what happens in Lust Vegas never stays there. Lust won't just stay in your head. It's like a cancer that, left unchecked, will multiply and spread. Sooner or later the thinking and the lusting and the imagining will lead to doing. The lust will have control over you instead of you controlling your feelings of lust. The occasional lustful thought can balloon into an obsession that later includes masturbation and fantasizing, and maybe even an actual affair. All of these thoughts and behaviors drive a wedge between you and your spouse that blocks intimacy.

Many wives especially have complained about their husbands' Internet porn addiction. It can be overwhelming. The availability of pornography is endless and always available—24/7/365. They feel as violated by the porn addiction as by an actual affair—maybe more. "I can fight against another woman coming between me and my husband," many women have said. "But how can I fight against something that's not even real, yet it's destroying my marriage?"

Be a Good Sex Steward

The Sexperiment opens the door to good sexual stewardship. Stewardship is simply the way we manage the things God has given to us. None of us is the owner of anything we have in life—not our time, our talent, or our treasure. We are all given those things by God to manage. That includes our sexuality.

You may be wondering how you could possibly be a good steward in the area of sex. It's like this: We all have unique abilities and aptitudes to be used while we're here on earth. We're all just stewards, and one day we are going to be held accountable concerning how we've handled the resources that God has given us. God has given unique gifts to us, and He wants us to return them to Him in their most developed fashion as an act of worship.

Our sexuality is a gift from God, and we are to steward it like any other gift He has given us. However, sex is unique in that it's multifaceted and multidimensional! God wants greatness from us in the sexual arena. Does that thought blow you away? It's God's design. Period. Honoring God's design for sexual intimacy—one man and one woman within the guidelines and guardrails of marriage—is being a good sex steward. As a good steward of God's gift of sexual intimacy, you will not allow lust to get past the guardrails of your marriage and threaten the bond you have with your spouse.

Joseph understood the concept of stewardship, even as Hotiphar was trolling for him, "day after day"* in fact. She had dropped all the guardrails around her marriage bed and was in hot, constant pursuit of Joseph. Bible scholars will tell you that Potiphar's wife tempted Joseph for about ten years. She was relentless. She didn't let up on her full-court press.

But Joseph respected the beauty of her marriage, even when she didn't. He refused to go to bed with her, despite her persistence. He said no. Every day. For ten years. A drop-dead gorgeous woman was after him every single day for ten years. And every single time he said no.

Was it because he was some superhuman, super-disciplined guy? Sometimes we want to think that the people in the Bible are somehow endowed with an extra measure of strength and forti-

---

* Genesis 39:10

tude. Joseph was a man's man, a human being. He was able to say no because of something better—the grace, the power, and the octane of the Lord. God gave him the strength...every day...for ten years. He refused even to be with her. Even today, Joseph's game plan is still a great strategy for staying out of Lust Vegas.

Develop a Proactive Strategy

Joseph's strategy for staying out of Lust Vegas was to simply stay away from his boss's wife. He ran! You also need a strategy for dealing with lust, because it can come up on you when you least expect it. Be proactive to keep it in check before it takes over. Lust does not play fair. If you're not proactive, sooner or later it will want to take over and start controlling you, your thoughts, and your actions.

Like lust gone out of control, adultery usually starts slowly and methodically. It follows a predictable path. There's an old folk tale that says if you drop a frog in a pan of boiling water, he'll immediately jump out. But if you put him in room temperature water and slowly keep turning up the heat, he'll boil to death because he won't realize when the water gets too hot. Most affairs take shape like that frog in the water—slowly. And as the heat intensifies, you'll find out that you've gone too far and can't get away from Lust Vegas.

Adultery happens frequently in the workplace, and it's no small wonder why. You begin spending a little extra time with an attractive co-worker. You look forward to those long, lingering lunches together. Somehow your conversation spills over into your personal life. He begins to share information about his marital frustrations. You may even mentally bring him into your bed while you're making love with your husband. You imagine it's him touching you, caressing you, kissing you. And no matter whether your husband is putting out his best moves, it's not good enough because your mind is on the guy at work.

That's why you simply cannot play with lust, like I couldn't play with the snake as a boy. I got bit. If you go to Lust Vegas to roll the dice and take a gamble, if you try to beat the house, you will lose *every time*. There's only one thing you can do when sexual temptation comes your way. Your only option is to leave Lust Vegas.

Joseph didn't allow lust to gain leverage in his life. He was a man who followed the Lord. He had lots of great qualities—a stand-up guy, a leader, a guy who moved from the pit to the pinnacle. He made it in spite of his adversities.

Imagine what might have happened if he'd taken Hotiphar up on her offer. Lust says, "You can do it just this once and no one will be the wiser." But lust always lies. Lust tells you no one will find out. Lust tells you that an affair would be beneficial to your marriage. Lust says if you don't have an affair, you'll probably end up getting a divorce.

That's just the enemy talking to you. He always wants to trick us out of enjoying God's best. The Evil One wanted to trick Joseph into missing out on God's best for his life. But God used Hotiphar's invitations to Lust Vegas as an opportunity to strengthen Joseph, to test him so he could emerge stronger and better.

Joseph was on his A-game. He kept his guard up against lust. When she caught him by his cloak and said, "Come to bed with me!" She was saying, "Let's do it right now." She wanted her invitation to seem like they could have a quick and easy secret tryst that her husband would never even know about, but Joseph was wise enough not to go there.

If you try to pet lust, eventually it's going to bite you. It'll keep hanging on and won't let go, just like the snake that bit me when I was a boy. Lust is not something to play with. That very thing that you chase for sexual freedom will end up incarcerating you. Because lust, being what it is, will bite you, no matter how carefully you try to handle it, no matter how discriminating you are in choosing it. Lust can't help but do what it does.

In the *Great Divorce*, author C. S. Lewis tells a great allegorical story about a ghost of a man afflicted by lust, represented by a red lizard that sits on the man's shoulder and whispers convincingly into his ear. The man eventually begins to despair about the lizard, at which point an angel offers to kill it for him. But the man is torn about what to do. The man fears the death of lust will kill him as well and makes excuses to the angel to keep the lizard. Finally, the man allows the angel to seize and kill the lizard. The angel grasps the reptile, breaks its neck, and throws it to the ground. Then the man is gloriously transformed into a real, solid being, while the lizard, rather than dying, is turned into a mighty stallion. Weeping with tears of joy, the man jumps onto the horse and they fly to the heavens.

How do we break the lust lizard's back? We do what Joseph did. When Hotiphar invited him to have sex with her, Joseph ran out of the house. He removed himself from the situation. He left Lust Vegas.

Pull Out Your Shun Gun

If you are going to have the kind of marriage that the Sexperiment invites you to have, you have to take lust off the table. There's no place for it within the context of marriage, so we need to avoid it in every temptation we face. And we never grow so strong in our faith or our marriages that the lure of lust is no longer an issue. The enemy is always trying to find ways to hit you at your weakest point.

The Evil One has a customized plan to take each of us out. What will take me out won't even be a temptation for you. One person can get taken out by a beautiful body in a thong bikini. Another person can get taken out by the sincere innocence and vulnerability of another person. A man might be attracted to a woman who would be more grateful than his wife for the things he would do for her.

But no matter what the enemy has designed to destroy your marriage, he just wants to mess you up and get you off the path of sexual stewardship. So we all have to be on guard... at all times... against sexual temptation.

So often when you see sexual temptation mentioned in the Bible, it is often associated with the word "flee," or God telling us about removing ourselves from the tempting encounter. That's how powerful, how multifaceted and multidimensional sexual temptation is.

What do you do when you face sexual temptation? What do you do when Potiphar's wife says, "Come to bed with me, have sex with me"? You've got to shun evil. You pull out your "shun gun" and flee.

For most of us, the temptation will come through our everyday associations. People usually commit adultery with friends—an attractive co-worker at the office or a neighbor whom you bump into frequently. You find reasons to spend time with this person—lunches at work or extended conversations while taking a walk through the neighborhood. You begin to make excuses to see this person.

The affair slowly begins to take shape and intensify. Then you begin to share things with this person that you shouldn't—feelings, marital problems, and vulnerabilities. Soon you form an emotional bond. Then it's just a matter of time before you are in bed with the person.

That's why you need to be very careful who your friends are. Your friends need to have the same depth of marital commitment, the same dedication to purity that you share with your spouse.

Be very careful about how you relate to your friends' spouses. Never relate to a friend's spouse without that friend being there or being within the context of your friendship. If you isolate the friendship with the friend's spouse and begin to share information and feelings that you shouldn't, you are playing with fire. You can't play with lust. Remember, if you roll the dice and gamble on lust, hoping that you can beat the house, you will lose every time.

Is there a Hotiphar in your life? Has lust lured you into its snare? What is that entity, that website, or that club that's saying to you, "Hey, come on in. After all, what happens in Lust Vegas stays in Lust Vegas." Whoever it is, whatever it is, you've got to flee. Resist the devil, and he will flee from you.*

---

* James 4:7

It's Never Too Late to Leave

A while back I had something wild happen to me. As a pastor, I meet interesting people all the time. But this was something that showed me it's never too late to leave Lust Vegas.

One day, my office received a phone call from the producer of a popular television show. He had seen our television program and was interested in one of the sermons I preached on sex.

When I picked up the phone, he said, "Hey, Ed, I think it's fascinating that you talk so openly about sex in church. I've never seen a preacher do that before."

Then he said something that caught me off guard. He said, "I was wondering if you would consider coming on our show. And we want you to talk to an adult film star about sex. I want you to give your opinion about what the Bible says about sex and sexuality. And then she wants to give her opinion, and she has a strong one, to you about her and her life in the adult film industry. We want to bring her to your church and have you guys sit down and have this open and honest conversation."

Well, I saw this great opportunity to share God's plan for sex and marriage with someone who obviously doesn't share the same view. It was a great opportunity to help someone living in Lust Vegas see that there is a greater plan out there. So, after talking to Lisa and some close friends, I decided to take the opportunity.

Later that week, I stood in our church with the cameras rolling and I watched this young girl, who is about the same age as our oldest daughter, walk in. And I saw her boyfriend/agent, who used to be a porn star, right there with her and all the fanfare with the limousine waiting out front. She walked in and we sat down. And as we began to talk, the producer butted in and said, "Excuse me, Ed, I've got to ask you this. What did you think about when you knew a porn star was coming to your church?"

I said, "That's easy. I was thinking, 'Isn't it great that we have a church that is open to everyone? Isn't it great where anyone can show up, even an adult film star, and they can hear God's plan for life, for marriage, for sex?'"

And for the next hour, I had an opportunity to talk to this girl about the reality of the porn industry, what God has to say about sex and marriage, and how, no matter what, God has a plan for people. And he can help people get out of Lust Vegas.

Then she began to give me the reasons and the rationale behind why she's in the adult film industry. She said, "Well, I help marriages. I help spice up sex lives. And I'm not hurting anybody.

"I'm a risk-taker. I like to walk on the edge. I'll do anything. And I'm making huge amounts of money. And that's just what I do."

And then she began to say, "How can you believe the Bible? I mean, the Bible was written by men. How can you say it's the word of God? I'm not sure that Jesus is the son of God."

And she began to fire questions like that and I began to explain to her about what the Bible says about some of these issues. I said, "You know what? You can ask any question you have. God is bigger than your doubt, bigger than your question, bigger than anything you want to throw at him. So bring it on."

As the conversation went on, I could tell she was searching. I told her, "Here's the real issue: You either go the way you're going, and I can tell you what's going to happen to you with amazing accuracy over the next several years. Or, you can do it Christ's way.

"Basically what you're doing, what the porn industry is doing, is taking sex out of context. You're taking a God-given gift and using it in a God-forbidden way.

"When someone looks at porn, or watches an adult film, they're stripping the humanity of the people they are watching perform sexual acts while they strip themselves of their humanity. But we're not animals! God doesn't want our lives to be lived that way. We're not hounds; we're humans. We're made in the image of God. And God wants us to use sex His way."

After talking with her for about an hour, I could tell that she was really struggling with her lifestyle and the things she was doing. She felt trapped in her very own Lust Vegas.

I said to her, "You know why you're here? We're not here for some television show. Sure, it'll be on one day. But do you know why you're really here? You're here because God has driven you here. You're here to hear God's truth."

She said, "Are you telling me I've got to quit the adult film industry?"

I said, "You know what I'm telling you? I'm telling you to give everything in your life to Jesus, because he has the greatest plan for your life. It's clear that you're seeking him. And Scriptures say when you seek him, he'll reveal himself to us. If you give your life to him, he'll take care of the rest. And yes, he will lead you out of that industry, out of Lust Vegas. I'm not saying today that if you pray this prayer—*boom!*—everything will be great. But I'm saying that if you want the best, if you want to discover how good God is, then give it all to Him."

And as this young girl stood to leave, with tears running down her cheeks, it was obvious that God was working on her heart. And when she walked out of the church, she turned to her boyfriend, who'd been in the porn business for a long time, and we heard her say, "What if he's right?" And I believe as she continues to seek God, He will help this girl leave Lust Vegas.

It's never too late to leave Lust Vegas. It doesn't matter where you are right now; God can help you leave that place and discover a place of purpose and passion, a place of true intimacy with your spouse.

Action Steps

1. Do an open and honest assessment of yourself before starting the Sexperiment. Are you living in Lust Vegas, or do you visit from time to time? Think about how lust has blocked intimacy in your marriage. If lust has blocked intimacy in your marriage, use the time you normally would have spent hanging out in Lust Vegas to think about how to please your spouse sexually.

2. Think about how you regard the issue of lust. Look at ways that you may be allowing lust to infiltrate your marriage—television, movies, magazines, the Internet...

3. Pack your bags and get out of Vegas! Get rid of everything that will tempt you—movies, magazines, photographs, etc. Place a filter on your Internet browser to restrict your access to certain websites. Pack up any distractions to intimacy within your marriage and throw them away.

4. Before you begin the Sexperiment, you and your spouse should spend some time flirting with each other, being romantic toward each other, and building your desire for each other without engaging in sex. Then, when you begin your week of sex, your focus will be on your spouse.

5. Think about the needs of your spouse. What gets him aroused? What turns her on? Take some preparation time before the Sexperiment to focus on the needs of your spouse and how you want to make love to your spouse.

—— *Before You Do* ——

*B*efore taking your vows is a good time to assess whether you are engaging in behaviors or thought patterns that will be a deterrent to building intimacy and closeness when you are married. If you're hanging out in Lust Vegas, you have to get out now if there is to be any hope for your marriage.

A woman called in to a radio talk show and complained that her husband liked to visit strip clubs. The DJ's comment on her situation was that the husband should be allowed to continue doing whatever he had been doing before they married. It's that kind of wacked-out advice that has marriages in trouble in this country. (And, as you might expect, the DJ was single.)

You probably have an expectation that the person you are about to marry will be totally into you. You should want that, but you also should be able to give that to the person you marry. The way you prepare for marriage is by making yourself the best person you can be prior to taking your vows.

Engagement is the time to prepare yourself for marriage. If you think it's OK to hang out in Lust Vegas because you haven't taken your vows yet, please think about that logic for a moment. You won't be able to automatically cut off that kind of behavior once you're married. If you're in Lust Vegas, whether in magazines, movies, or the Internet, the time to get out of there is now so that you can take your vows giving your marriage 100 percent of yourself.

——— *The Yoke Is Not a Joke* ———

*A*re you thinking that you can do whatever you like because you're single and not in a relationship that could lead to marriage? If you are thinking that way, please stop right there.

If you are hanging out in Lust Vegas, believing that it's OK as long as you're not actually having sex, think about how much more productive you could be if you invested that time and energy into something Godly, something positive. I'm not saying you have to read the Bible 24/7, but I am saying that you need to be proactive to keep your heart and mind out of Lust Vegas.

But as a matter of fact, reading the Bible is a great place to start when you're trying to leave Lust Vegas. God's Word is a wonderful tool for strengthening us in mind, body, and spirit. Reading a contemporary version can help you understand God's wisdom better and apply it to your life and your dating decisions.

It's hard, if not impossible, to know anyone's thoughts and secret behaviors. Pray and ask God to give you wisdom and insight about the people you date. Then don't ignore the truth He reveals to you about someone you're interested in or dating. Be wise enough to look beyond a pretty face, a muscular body, or a good income and see the person God reveals.

7

Trust Funds Are Nothing

While I was in a pet store looking for a particular type of dog collar, a woman in her mid-fifties started a conversation with me about different collars.

After we talked for a few minutes, she asked, "What do you do for a living?"

"I'm a pastor."

"Really?" she said. "I'm not religious."

I said, "I'm not either. I'm about a relationship with Jesus, but I'm not religious."

Then she asked, "What do you talk about at your mass or the thing that you do?"

I said, "Recently, I've been talking about divorce."

When I said that, she got a strange look on her face and said, "Divorce? That will _____ up your life." She added, "I left my husband ten years ago, and someone should have taken my _____ and tied me to a tree and beat the _____ out of me."

I could feel her hurt even though it had been a decade since she and her husband split, and I experienced some of the venom through her choice of words.

She shared more. "My daughter called me just a couple days ago and said, 'Mom, our family isn't normal. You're here; dad is over there. Everything is totally screwed up.'"

And then she looked at me and said, "You know what? My daughter was right. When you talk about divorce, you tell people the grass is never greener. And you tell these husbands and wives to look past the now."

Wow! Those are powerful words about marriage from a person who's not into religion or church.

After I got my dog collar, I started thinking, what if that lady could go back ten years in her marriage? What if she could go back to the moment just before she put her hand on the doorknob to walk out on her marriage? What if she could go back and understand what pushed her through the door of divorce?

It's interesting to me that this woman's daughter was an adult, but she was still adversely affected by her parents' divorce. When a marriage breaks up, it affects the two spouses, but the devastation reaches much further—friends, neighbors, church members, parents, siblings . . . but especially children and grandchildren.

We want to help as many people as possible avoid the kind of pain this woman and her family have experienced and instead move toward God's dynamic design! That's why Lisa and I are promoting the Sexperiment. Maybe if that woman and her husband had taken a Sexperiment challenge eleven years before I had that conversation with her, they might have taken divorce off the table as an option and drawn closer together. Her family might have remained intact instead of being scattered the way her daughter indicated. If they'd had a Sexperiment, maybe they would have left their children a legacy that included forgiveness, reconciliation, and intimacy rather than one of hurt and regret.

How Deep Is Your Footprint?

As responsible parents, Lisa and I have made provisions for our children in case of our demise. But as important as it is to provide for their future financial well-being, we're also leaving them something far greater. We believe the greatest legacy we are leaving our children is not with our bank account or an insurance policy or even with our worldwide ministry. The greatest footprint we will stamp on our family is the model of a solid foundation in marriage.

Long after they are grown and gone, our children will remember that their parents have a loving relationship that includes physical intimacy. Our marriage will be their model by which to set the standard in choosing a life partner. That's the deepest footprint we can stamp upon our children's future.

Most people want to leave their footprint on the world. They want to make a difference in the lives of those around them. And they try everything to do that—from establishing a strong financial portfolio for their children's future to investing time in the community to ensure society remembers them.

But one of the greatest ways to establish a legacy is to have a great sex life in marriage. As the sex goes in marriage, so goes the rest of the marriage. So goes the marriage, so goes the family. So goes the family, so goes society. There's no greater gift you can give the next generation or society at large than the model of a strong and lasting marriage.

Why is sex such an important factor in the marital fulfillment equation? Research has shown that married couples with a strong sex life have a stronger marriage and greater fulfillment. Marital satisfaction and sexual satisfaction are inextricably connected.

This kind of fulfillment doesn't usually just happen. When it does occur in marriages, it's usually because both spouses have taken specific steps to ensure their marital stability, intimacy, and fulfillment. There are some factors to consider as you initiate your Sexperiment and then take it beyond for ongoing marital satisfaction. These are keys to unlock the doors to greater intimacy in marriage and an influential legacy for your children.

Be a Parent CEO

Our country has been rocked by corporate scandals. It's not even shocking anymore. One after another, billion-dollar corporations have folded and caused many innocent lives to collapse right along with them.

These corporations looked great on the outside, with beautiful buildings and glowing annual reports. On the inside, though, they were riddled with lies, greed, and corruption. From technology to securities to energy, all of those failed companies had something in common— they were led by CEOs who should not have been corporate heads.

When those corporations failed, lives were devastated right along with them. People lost their entire savings and investment portfolios. They had saved and planned for a secure future, but because of corporate irresponsibility, they had no financial legacy.

But as bad as those major scandals were—Enron, WorldCom, Madoff Investment Securities—there is an even bigger scandal that is devastating families across the nation. I'm talking about the scandal in the family corporate structure.

The family scandal occurs the moment the obstetrician slaps your baby on the bottom and you hear your newborn's first cry. The moment that occurs, the baby looks at the cushy family corporate chair and says, "I am going to do a hostile takeover."

Immediately after the first baby is born, the parents allow themselves to be moved from executive staff positions into support staff positions. The kids move from the support staff role into the executive staff position. Once they become CEOs, once their little behinds feel the leather of that chair in the corner office, once they look at the view, once they fly in the corporate jet, and once they experience the parties and the perks, the parents are no longer in control. It's a hostile takeover.

How does this affect the legacy you leave to your children? In a number of households, the kids are running the show. We make jokes about kids calling the shots, but it's not funny, because the effects are not pretty.

When kids are running the family business and become the primary focus of the marriage, it's like putting your marriage on life support. The relationship will be sustained as long as the two of you are plugged into the children. But what happens when they leave? So many marriages end after their kids are grown and gone because the husband and wife failed to build a relationship with each other. The ones they built the relationship with are now gone. What's worse, they left without a legacy of a loving, lasting marriage.

If your kids are calling the shots in your marriage because they've done a hostile takeover, you need to regain control, starting with your Sexperiment week. As the parents, you need to take over—move back into the corner office, sit down and run the show, speak the truth in love.

Parents have to be parents. It is our responsibility to cast vision for the family. And to do that, we have to have the marriage be the most important priority of the family.

Why are a bunch of kids running the show in homes across America? It's basically because we're all selfish. We all have this desire to control, and kids show this desire at strikingly young ages.

But another reason why a lot of parents usher their kids into the CEO role is because they're detached. They don't want to mess with it. Parents want to do the Heisman Trophy thing and stiff-arm their responsibility away.

Too many parents today are trying to be a friend to their children rather than a parent. But kids need the structure and stability of parents who are in charge. Kids complain when they don't get their way, but the truth is they get great comfort from knowing that someone older and wiser is calling the shots.

Some parents allow their kids to take over because they believe what the culture says—that kids who talk back to and manipulate their parents are cute. They even become famous for doing it on television.

But the greatest lie of our culture is that the kids are the nucleus of the family cell. That is ludicrous. It's not biblical, and it's just plain wrong.

The *marriage* is the nucleus of the family cell. If you know anything about science and biology, you know that the nucleus is the power that gives a cell the ability to relate to other cells. The same is true in the parent-CEO home.

A lot of parents are missing out on marital fulfillment because the kids are calling the shots. Kids have their parents running around so much that Mom and Dad don't have time or energy for making love.

In a *Newsweek* magazine article about sexless marriages, one parent named Ann, a thirty-nine-year-old lawyer with two kids, shared frustration that so many parents have. When she and her husband were first married, they had sex almost every day. Everything changed after their daughter was born.

By the time the child was five years old, she started coming into their bedroom every night. Pretty soon, the dog started whining to get on the bed too. "At 3 or 4 a.m., I kick my husband out for snoring and he ends up sleeping in my daughter's princess twin bed with the Tinkerbell night light blinking in his face," Ann said. "So how are we supposed to have sex?"*

That kind of hostile kid takeover is a major killer of marital intimacy.

Parents are supposed to run the show and call the shots. Starting with the Sexperiment week, your children can start to learn what it means to be support staff, not CEOs, because you and your spouse will put each other at the center of the family. As a husband and wife first, and as parents second, you will make intimacy and time alone a priority. You say when, where, and how, and the kids just have to fall in line with what you have decided.

Take the leadership role, demote your kids, and do what you

---

* http://www.newsweek.com/2003/06/29/we-re-not-in-the-mood.html

should do. Now, realize that when you have this exchange of roles, and your kids move from the executive corner office into the support staff role, they're not going to be happy. They will probably rebel, and one of you will want to fold. What should you do?

The number-one thing you should do is keep your eye on God's agenda. Keep in mind God's plan and design for marriage. The second thing you should do is recommit to the marital relationship. After you align these first two things, then comes number three—expect conflict.

Why conflict? Because by now your kids have been sitting in the big CEO chair for years and years. They like the spotlight. They like leading the way, and they are not going to resign without a fight. But remember, as a parent, you're the leader. Stick together and don't give in. Something far more important than your child's temper tantrum will be at stake—your marriage and your legacy, which will greatly influence their future.

Believe me, your kids would much rather be snatched out of the big CEO chair than to have their parents living in separate households because they're divorced.

Family Shareholder Meeting

To regain your position as CEO, you will need to have a family shareholder meeting. This is not a board meeting, mind you, because your kids aren't on the board of directors. You and your spouse are the only two family members who constitute the board. You are the co-chairpersons of the board.

Now, your family, your kids, do have some stock in the family company at stake. But it's not some 50/50 parents-versus-kids deal here. To get back into the corner office, you and your spouse should sit down with your family team, your shareholders, and cast the vision to them. Let them see that, as the parents, you work together to call the shots.

The Family Vision

The Bible says that where there is no vision, the people will perish.* So, you should have a vision, a mission for your family. If you don't have a vision, your family will perish to the influences and temptations the enemy has designed to tear families apart.

Now, you may be saying, "That's cool, Ed. I guess we'd better try to formulate a vision for our family. Um, what should that be? I don't know."

You don't have to worry about your vision. Just chill, because the vision is already laid out for you in the Bible. Here's what Joshua said about his family: "As for me and my household, we will serve the Lord."†

Joshua didn't take a vote. He didn't consult *Robert's Rules of Order*. He didn't put together a focus group, think tank, or committee. He made a declaration regarding what his family would do. Basically, he said, "I'm the parent. I'm calling the shots. We're going to follow the Lord." He cast the vision for his family.

Once you cast your vision for your family, you have to do something else. You have to *build* the vision. You have to strap that vision to commitment, endurance, and the stuff needed to carry it through. I know a lot of men and women who talk vision all day and night, but they have never *done* the stuff to bring it to fruition. We've got to do the stuff.

I challenge you to do something Lisa and I started doing a long time ago with our kids. Often, we will give our four children goals. Then we are there as consultants to help them understand how to achieve those goals. That's what it means to be a CEO in the family. We set the goals, not our kids.

If you don't have leadership, in the family or anywhere else, a vacuum exists in the place where leadership should be. Whenever you have a leadership vacuum, guess who begins to lead. People who are clueless about leadership step up to lead, like kids.

---

* Proverbs 29:18, NKJV
† Joshua 24:15

You may have seen kids like that. They have parents who, for whatever reason, have abdicated their parental responsibility—perhaps because they're overworked or substance abusers—and a kid is left in charge. They're getting younger siblings ready for school. They're making meals for the family. They're trying to support the family mentally and emotionally, and that's something a child is not equipped to do.

Making the Transition

Moving from being kid-centered to marriage-centered means making some adjustments in your relationship. You and your spouse may have to learn how to relate to each other intimately all over again. But it's worth it. The best thing you can do for your kids is to have a great marriage. If you don't, your kids will never launch from your home with great projection.

So, what do you do to have a great marriage? Take time to connect—relationally, sexually, and emotionally. The Bible says, "For this reason a man shall leave his father and mother and be joined to his wife, and they shall become one flesh."* That's superglue holding your marriage together.

The Sexperiment was created for couples who have neglected to connect in a way that is fulfilling to them. Your week of sexual intimacy will get you and your spouse engaged in physical closeness, but during that week you also will begin to see other neglected or empty spaces in your marriage. It is your opportunity to realign your relationship to reconnect with your spouse for lasting intimacy that spells L-E-G-A-C-Y.

To get a glimpse of what a great marriage looks like, there has to be more than physical intimacy. You need to connect with each other in ways that inspire intimacy. Engage in the nonsexual things during the day that can translate to sexual arousal at night.

---

* Genesis 2:24

It takes work to cleave, to be joined. It doesn't just happen because you have a wedding.

Honor

After the word *love,* the word *honor* is the second component of the traditional vows that we commit to in marriage. Husbands and wives vow to honor each other.

Do you know how to honor your spouse? You can honor each other in specific ways through deliberate acts.

The most immediate way to honor your spouse is by showing respect, both publicly and privately. Not all spouses do that. Some show public respect, but denigrate their spouse privately.

For instance, a woman praises her husband in public, but when they are at home, she often yells at him or calls him names when speaking to him.

Her husband does the opposite. He speaks civilly to his wife at home, but in public he often disrespects her. His rudeness toward her is rooted in a distorted need to demonstrate to others that he is the head of his household.

Respect is an important part of honoring your spouse, because if you don't have that, you can't have unfettered intimacy. You can't have the openness and vulnerability that genuine intimacy requires because the disrespected person will always have a wall of protection around them, even if they don't realize it.

We'll discuss respect a bit more later in this chapter, but there are other important ways to honor your spouse that can go a long way in adding a bit of incentive in the bedroom—affirmation and admiration.

Affirmation

What does it mean when I affirm something? It's a statement that I exert about the existence of something. So when I affirm Lisa, I say something like, "Lisa, you're a great cook."

And she really is. That's a fact. But just because it's a fact, it doesn't mean I should never affirm her gifts. Every now and then I just tell her, "Lisa, you're an awesome chef."

Many times she'll tell me, "Ed, I really like the way you handled that situation." We all need affirmation.

Admiration

Admiration is when we are enthusiastically approving of something. We all need admiration, no matter how accomplished we are. No matter how much money an actor makes in movies, he wants the admiration of his peers in the form of an Academy Award. No matter how accomplished a singer is, she longs for the admiration of her peers in the form of a Grammy.

Often people come up to me after a worship service and say, "Ed, I enjoyed that talk. That really meant a lot to me, and God really used you." I love those words of affirmation and admiration.

Sometimes people preface their comments with, "Well, Ed, I know you must hear this all the time, but..."

Actually, I don't hear that all the time. I appreciate hearing from people, whether after church or by e-mail, telephone, or text message, that I've been able to help them. They really put wind in my sail because, after all, that's what I've been called to do.

But there is one person who can take affirmation and admiration in my life to a 'hole 'nutha level. Lisa. When my wife affirms and admires me by saying something like, "Honey, I loved today's message," that just does it for me!

The Bible says that words are like jewelry: "A word aptly spoken is like apples of gold in settings of silver."*

Study your spouse. Know what puts wind in your husband's or wife's sail. A touch, a look, a comment...that's TLC. We have got to be about affirmation and admiration.

During your Sexperiment week, pay careful attention to ways

---

* Proverbs 25:11

you can honor your spouse by showing him or her an extra measure of respect, affirmation, and admiration.

The Sexperiment is about taking your marriage relationship to a new level—a 'hole 'nutha level! So this is the time to step up your game and honor your spouse like never before.

As you step up your game, your children will take notice. As they see you being more respectful, affirming, and admiring toward each other, they will witness a new paradigm for marriage relationships. It will inspire them to set higher standards for their own marriage someday.

A strong marriage is a legacy to which no trust fund can compare. But I must warn you, in order to accomplish this, you have to set some priorities.

It's good to tell your children that your marriage is important. But when your children observe firsthand that their parents' marriage is important because you prioritize spending time together, that gives them a totally different understanding of covenant marriage.

When your children see that the two of you enjoy spending time together and that you make it a priority, it teaches them that the husband-wife relationship is the highest priority in the family. It teaches them that Mom and Dad love each other with a special kind of love, a love that is reserved for each other only. It teaches them that even though Mom and Dad go out or go away to be alone together, they will come back happier and stronger.

Prioritize Marriage

I love the word *priority* because of the root word *prior.* We need to set the priority *prior* to engaging in an activity. A lot of us aren't living priority-driven lives. We're letting the "-ities" of life throw us off track and off focus, focus that should be on God, marriage, and kids.

Instead, we say, "Oh, I've got this '-ity,' that '-ity,' and that '-ity.' I'll just make a decision when the '-ity' hits me." No, no, no! You make your decisions about how to invest your time *prior* to the "-ity"!

You don't say, "Well, here is the activity. OK, I wonder what my priorities are?" No, before committing to or engaging in any activity, know your priorities: God, marriage, kids.

Ask yourself, "Does this activity encroach upon my development in my relationship with God? Does it encroach upon my marriage? Does it encroach upon my children?" You have to ask yourself those hard questions.

Let me share something with you that I've learned about setting priorities. Lisa and I live pretty busy lives. We are both authors. We have four kids—LeeBeth, EJ, Laurie, and Landra—who are involved in a lot of extracurricular activities.

As pastor of Fellowship Church in Dallas/Fort Worth and Miami, every weekend I speak at multiple worship services. I have to have fresh material to talk about and get "prayed up" to share a message from the Word of God. To prepare for my sermons, I have to write a term paper—that's about twenty pages of research. I have to read books, listen to recordings, talk to people, and anything else I need to do to make the message relevant and inspiring. I also do some traveling and speaking at other events.

Lisa and I enjoy having busy lives and we love the ministry that we have. But sometimes, with all of that activity there are bound to be schedule conflicts.

I remember one time, in the midst of all our professional and family obligations, our date night was kind of up in the air because we were scheduled to attend an activity that was pretty important. The activity was a good thing, and we did need to be there. It was one of those things where, if we didn't show up, someone would say, "You know, Ed, you and Lisa really should have been there."

But instead of assuming we simply had to be at this important event, Lisa and I decided to stop and prioritize. We realized that we hadn't had a date night for several weeks. And since our marriage is the second most important thing in the world to us, we decided to honor that time for ourselves. See, in our world, God is number one. Number two is the marriage. Number three is the kids.

Setting priorities means saying yes to the best. The best thing is God, because God wants the best for you. But in order to say yes to the best, you have to say no to the good. Remember, good is the enemy of best.

In the three decades that Lisa and I have been together, I've made many decisions where I have not made the right call. I've let activities or something else, another "-ity," mess up the structure of God, marriage, and kids. But the more I prioritize and put the best first, it gets easier to make the right call.

Vulnerability

Prioritizing your time together as a couple is important, but what you do during that time together is equally important. The reason why I strongly promote date night and weekend getaways—spouses spending time in a chosen venue where you draw away from everything else—is because it promotes vulnerability.

Being alone in a neutral venue with your spouse is a place where you can be vulnerable and share your fears, your dreams, your questions, and your desires.

Vulnerability and intimacy are intrinsically tied together. When I'm vulnerable with Lisa and when she's vulnerable with me, we share our fears, our dreams, our successes, our questions, and our failures.

As you engage in the Sexperiment, I challenge you to create venues of vulnerability. You can't have vulnerability on the fly. You can't have vulnerability when you're overcommitted, overstimulated, and living over-the-top, because you're following an agenda that someone else has set for you, especially your kids.

Kids are critical when it comes to vulnerability. Earlier I defined the word "kids" as an acronym: Keeping Intimacy at a Distance Successfully. So if you want to have those venues of vulnerability, you better keep your kids at a distance successfully. Remember, spouses stay, kids leave. And as they leave, you want them to go with the legacy of a loving, affectionate, intimate marriage that you have modeled for them.

Your kids should see the fruit of your vulnerability in marriage, but your vulnerability itself should not be visible to them—or anyone else, for that matter. So here's an important point to remember: Don't take your vulnerability and make it visible.

This isn't as much of a problem for men, because vulnerability doesn't come naturally to us. It is very tempting for women to do this, however, because women speak thousands more words a day than men.

Women are far more comfortable sharing their feelings, insecurities, and vulnerabilities. So it's very tempting for women to talk about times of vulnerability with girlfriends over lunch or in aerobics class or while shopping together, or even with their kids. But that's definitely a boundary you don't want to cross. If your boundary lines with your children have a bunch of holes or gray areas, that's dangerous for your marriage.

Save your vulnerabilities for your spouse. Talk to your spouse. Talk to God. Talk to a Christian counselor or maybe even to a pastor about it. When you reserve your vulnerability for the right place, your words will be like apples of gold in settings of silver. And that's quite a valuable legacy to leave your children.

Respect

Contempt is a pretty tough word. It's a lack of respect or reverence for something. The covenant of marriage—a blood bond for life—is all about respect. It's about vulnerability. It's about affirmation. It's about admiration. So instead of defensiveness, try vulnerability. Instead of contempt, try respect.

I can tell if a marriage is lacking in respect by observing how the wife watches her husband when he talks. If he's talking and she's looking at him like she's disgusted, or she corrects everything he says, I can tell they're headed for marital trouble if they're not there already. Spouses often disrespect each other and feel like they were pushed into it, like they can't help it. But they can.

Several years ago I was calling dog breeders looking for a bull-mastiff. One breeder I spoke to told me, "I would love for you to have one of our bullmastiffs. In fact, our dog Sadie is going to have babies very soon. Ed, I wish you could see her right now." And then she started talking to the dog like she was a baby: "You're going to be a good mommy, aren't you, Sadie? Such a good girl..."

All of a sudden, she goes from baby-talking the dog to yelling at her husband. "What do you want? Shut up! I'm on the phone. Ed, I'm sorry my husband interrupted our conversation..." She was treating Sadie the dog better than her spouse. Isn't that amazing?

What kind of legacy are you leaving if your kids see that you talk to the dog better than you talk to your mate? You should talk to your spouse respectfully, because you're one flesh. So when you disrespect your spouse, you're disrespecting yourself. Follow what the Bible says: "Do nothing out of selfish ambition or vain conceit, but in humility consider others [your spouse] better than yourselves."*

Reconciliation

That Bible verse is good to remember when conflict arises in your relationship. Anytime Lisa and I have a relational sticking point—an

---

* Philippians 2:3

argument, a problem, or when I've done something against her—as a follower of Christ, I believe I have a responsibility to quickly reconcile with her because I've been greatly and perfectly reconciled by Jesus Christ.

Lisa and I work to reconcile quickly because it's the right thing to do and it blesses our marriage, but we also are aware that we are modeling reconciliation for our children as part of our legacy to them.

As a father and a pastor, I'm well aware that I can't talk about reconciliation to my children on Sundays in church but not live it in my marriage to their mother. They're learning how to practice reconciliation in their relationships by watching us.

Before our three youngest children were old enough to drive, several days a week I would take them to school. Like most kids, ours would argue and fight in the car. Most of the time, I could stand about five minutes of their bickering. Then I would tell them, "Stop! Not another word until we get to school. OK?"

"Yes, sir," they would respond, and for a while all you would hear was the hum of the car engine.

Whenever we went a certain route to their school, we would always go over a bridge. Invariably, on the bridge, one of the kids would ask, "Dad, can I say something?"

I'd say (for example), "Yes, Laurie."

"Landra, I am sorry. Will you forgive me?"

And then maybe the next week it would be, "Laurie, will you forgive me?"

The week after that, "EJ, will you forgive me?" It always happened on the bridge.

So I started calling that spot the Bridge of Forgiveness. Whenever we go over the bridge, I know forgiveness will take place.

I think marriages need a bridge of forgiveness. It's the point where enough bickering is enough. You have a chance to think it over, and when you get to the bridge of forgiveness, you want to be reconciled and you take steps to do so.

Husbands and wives need to travel on the bridge of forgiveness regularly—daily, weekly, monthly, annually—and have a ministry of grace and reconciliation in their own home that their children want to emulate.

Trust Funds Are Nothing

Trust funds can be an important piece of any parent's legacy to their children, but it's not the most important thing. A legacy of a loving, intimate marriage can influence your children's lives in far greater ways than a trust fund can.

Many famous so-called trust-fund babies (aka "trustafarians") regularly make headlines for their wild and crazy antics. They're living on wealth that someone provided for them, but they are missing something far more valuable than money. So many of them got the money, but they didn't receive the legacy of loving, committed parents who modeled the intimacy of covenantal marriage.

I learned a long time ago that the best thing I can do for my kids is to work on my marriage. When I love Lisa as Christ loved the Church, I am doing the very best thing for our children. I also discovered that when I express selfishness to Lisa, I am eroding my children's self-esteem.

So goes your marriage, so go your kids. So goes your marriage, so goes your parenting. So goes your marriage, so goes the foundation and the self-esteem and the confidence of your kids. So goes your marriage, so goes the trajectory of your kids when they leave home to live their own lives.

If you are worried about your kids' future, then worry about your marriage. And do what you can to work on that relationship. There is no better investment you can make in the success of your kids than a healthy and stable marriage.

Give the Sexperiment a try and see how this creating-a-legacy stuff works for seven days. As you reap the benefits, you will want to continue on the path that leaves a solid legacy on which your children can build their own relational future.

Action Steps

1. Write a "last will and testament" to your children that contains the relationship lessons you will leave them based on the quality of your marriage. For example: "We, John and Mary, leave our children with the understanding that the marriage is a covenant relationship." Or "We leave them a spirit of joy between husband and wife that will show them that marriage is the best relationship they can have on earth." After you have written down about ten things, discuss them with your spouse. Talk about ways that you can leave a strong legacy for your children through your marriage.

2. As you prepare for your Sexperiment, think about the "-ities" that can interfere with your week of intimacy. Make a list with your spouse of the "-ities" that block intimacy in your marriage. Discuss what it means to prioritize and put God first, marriage second, and kids third. How does that look in your marriage?

3. Create a list of seven ways you can honor your spouse through affirmation and admiration during the Sexperiment week. Choose one each day of the Sexperiment to help build intimacy in your marriage.

4. Before you begin the Sexperiment, talk with your children and ask them to share their perceptions about your marriage. Then ask yourselves, does your marriage inspire your children to want the kind of marriage you have someday? Discuss their feedback with your spouse in private to help you know the kind of legacy you are leaving your children. Then talk about how you hope the Sexperiment will help you build a stronger legacy for them.

——————— *Before You Do* ———————

*I*n an average year, there will be 2.3 million marriages in America. Yet almost half of first marriages will end in divorce. Second marriages fare even worse—67 percent of them end up in the deep weeds. And if you think practice makes perfect, you're wrong, because 74 percent of third marriages don't make it.

It's paradoxical. On one hand, we're rushing to the altar. On the other hand, we're rushing to divorce court. Yet we still take the time to build a relationship with someone, hoping that it will lead to marriage.

Regardless of whether you come from a home where your parents divorced or your parents stayed together, now is the time for you to consider what you learned about marriage while growing up in your family.

It's important for you to look at those factors because they will affect how you relate to your spouse. Did you see a loving, nurturing, supportive relationship? Perhaps you came from a loving home where your parents demonstrated covenant marriage but your future spouse was raised by divorced parents. How do you come to the same place regarding marriage as a covenantal relationship?

Hopefully you and your fiancé will seek Christian counseling before you marry to help you flesh out these issues. Your counselor will help you understand how you can set your priorities—God, marriage, and children—in your relationship and implement them effectively.

No matter the circumstances under which you will marry, resolve that the two of you will serve God, and that your marriage will always be your most important relationship on earth. Set your priorities accordingly.

————— *The Yoke Is Not a Joke...* —————

$\mathscr{A}$fter reading this chapter, you may be thinking, "Wow! This marriage stuff is a lot of work. When you involve kids, it really becomes serious stuff." And you would be right.

Perhaps in reading these chapters you can begin to see how couples get off track and why they need a Sexperiment week to help them reconnect and realign their relationship.

After reading this book, think about some of the married couples you know. Think about the characteristics of their marriages that left an impression upon you, good or bad. What makes the good marriage good? What makes the weak marriages weak? Are they leaving a strong legacy for their children?

These are important observations to make because you will want to find these same characteristics in anyone you date.

So many people date a look or an image, rather than a person, only to be disappointed when they marry and their spouse prioritizes a career, their parents' needs, or even a golf game more than the marriage.

People don't magically change once they say "I do." Don't be mesmerized by dating an image and lose perspective on what's really important for marriage. The person you see while you're dating will be the same person you see in bed every night as husband and wife.

It's important to date people who demonstrate the potential to put God first, marriage second, and kids third. It's important to date a person who wants to leave the legacy of a good marriage relationship and understands why it's so important.

8

Pillow Talk

$\mathcal{T}$he first time I laid eyes on Lisa was at church in Columbia, South Carolina. I was sitting in the balcony, maybe the second row from the back. All my friends were saying, "Wow! Look at that girl. Man, she's hot!"

Several weeks later, a friend of ours, David "Bubbles" Swindler, sent me a note that said, "Lisa would really love it if you would give her a call." I really wanted to talk to her, but Lisa has always been kind of poised and mature acting. So, I was a little bit nervous about calling her. But I did call, and we connected from the first time we talked.

Lisa: Ed called me on a Monday night. I guess he'd got the note on Sunday. I didn't know David sent him that note, but when he called I was running through the house, out of breath because I couldn't find my tennis shoes and I was late for a softball game. I was even more out of breath when I heard his voice at the other end. I was so excited that he'd called. It was the first of many, many great phone calls.

Ed: A little while later we had our first date, so to speak. We went to the theater at Richland Mall and saw *Jaws*.

Lisa: That's actually where we held hands the first time.

Ed: Yeah, it was during the scene when they shot the barrel in the shark.

Lisa: Actually, it was pinkies. While we were getting to know each other, we'd talk on the phone all the time. Once Ed could drive, we started going out on dates.

Ed: I guess we had been dating for maybe two or three months when my family went to Jamaica on a two-week trip.

Lisa: It felt like he was going for six months. And we were just devastated that we were going to be apart.

Ed: While my family and I were away, Lisa sent me a six-page letter with Charlié perfume sprayed on the paper. My parents kept teasing me, "What does Lisa have to say? Why don't you read the letter to us?" I was embarrassed to read it aloud because it said, "I love you and blah, blah, blah."

Lisa: Then Ed sent me back a letter with Jovan Musk Oil on it.

Those were the days when Lisa and I could spend hours communicating with each other, verbally and nonverbally. But as good as those times were, even in our dating days, we had some struggles with communication. By and large, though, it was good. I think it's so cool how God brought our relationship full circle: On June 26, 1982, at First Baptist Church of Columbia, South Carolina, we became husband and wife.

When I think back to the early days of our relationship, I think it's great that communication was such a priority for us. I firmly believe dating couples who seek the Lord daily and communicate with him regularly are going to communicate in their marriage in magnificent ways.

Being in ministry now for all these years and being married for almost three decades, Lisa and I have had the opportunity to talk to a lot of couples. It's staggering to think about the communication breakdowns and problems that so many husbands and wives deal with.

Most couples start out like Lisa and I did when we were dating. When a guy and a girl date, everything—especially communication—just flows. It seems so easy and effortless, doesn't it? Do you remember hours-long telephone conversations, long walks, and the two of you closing down restaurants because you couldn't get enough of talking with each other?

Then the moment the pastor pronounced you husband and wife, you expected communication to deepen, didn't you? You still expected those long, deep conversations and romantic talks. You still expected the long walks. You still expected to be closing down restaurants.

But something changed after you said your vows. Conversation became a little tired, a little predictable, and a little stale. After a few years of marriage, you've heard the same stories so many times that you could recite them from memory. Your talks may have turned from dreams, desires, plans, and promises, to one- and two-word sound bites of reality. Maybe, just maybe, your communication (talking and listening) skills aren't quite what they used to be when you got married.

I think a key reason why couples have such a challenging time communicating at certain junctures in marriage is because men and women are so different. Of course, the physical differences are obvious. And we've discussed in chapter two some of the differences between men's and women's intimacy needs. But men and women communicate differently too. We also communicate differently about sex and sexual needs. You can't have intimacy (aka "into me, see") without communication.

Communication happens in relationships, both verbal and nonverbal. Whether it's positive or negative, good or bad, depends on you.

Addressing communication issues is critical to having the great sex life you hope to spark during the Sexperiment. Maybe you're thinking, "Ed, there's not a lot of talk going on during sex, so what's the point?" There may not be a lot of talking going on during sex, but there's lots of communication going on. And it starts before couples ever make it anywhere near the bedroom.

We know that men and women don't communicate in the same way. But why is it so hard sometimes for men and women to communicate?

Let's say, for example, a woman goes to get her hair done. She runs into a female friend, who will say something like, "Oh, girl!

Your hair looks great! That's a new color, isn't it?" Then the woman with the new hairdo will respond, "Thanks. It's a little lighter than I wanted, but it's starting to grow on me." They may go on and on about the new hairdo.

Conversely, if a man gets a haircut, his friend will ask, "Haircut?" And the man will respond, "Yeah." End of conversation.

How does good communication happen in marriage when women speak 12,000 more words a day than men do?

God created men and women differently, but we still have to communicate in order to get along. So how do we share in the kind of vital exchange needed to establish or maintain the intimacy that strong marriages need? How do we share our hopes, dreams, and expectations when women like to communicate using lots of words while men tend to keep it short and to the point?

Here's a starting point:

*"A word fitly spoken and in due season is like apples of gold in a setting of silver."**

The right words at the right time can really make a difference. It is a priceless gift of great value.

There are times to speak and times to remain silent. While it's true that issues in marriage have to be dealt with, it takes maturity and consideration to know when to speak. You have to really get into your spouse, get to know him or her to know the times when he or she can't hear you.

I am naturally a night owl and Lisa is naturally a morning person. And here is what we have come to as a compromise. We have established our own time zone. I go to bed earlier than I normally would, and she goes to bed later than she normally would. We now have our own time zone, when we are alert, geared up, and ready to communicate. When you and your spouse find your time-zone sweet spot, you'll find that your ability to communicate will be at its peak. Let me encourage you to do some time-zone work.

---

* Proverbs 25:11, NRSV

"*Everyone should be quick to listen, slow to speak and slow to become angry.*"*

If you do more listening than talking, I can guarantee that your marriage will move toward the kind of intimacy you're hoping to initiate through the Sexperiment. If you're listening to your spouse more than talking, that means you're more into your spouse. It means you're listening to his or her needs, wants, and desires, like you did before you married. It means you're prioritizing your spouse's needs over your own. It means intimacy (into me, see).

"*Don't use foul or abusive language. Let everything you say be good and helpful, so that your words will be an encouragement to those who hear them.*"†

Every couple should have some "don't go there" rules regarding communication, even in teasing or humor. There should be a zone you just don't enter, in order to maintain respect toward each other. If you're using foul or abusive language toward your spouse, you're destroying any possibility for authentic intimacy in your marriage.

I grew up with a bunch of guys in Canton, North Carolina. One of them was a great guy named Mike. We used to play at his house often. One of the good things about playing at Mike's house was the fact that no matter what sport we played—baseball, football, or whatever—he would always lay out the rules before we played.

He'd always say, "OK, Ed. If you go here, that's out of bounds near that tree. If you hit a ball this way, if you go over that fence, or if it goes to the left by the house, that's a foul ball. If you hit it there, that's a home run." So when I was playing with Mike, I always knew what the rules were.

Now, I also hung out with a few other guys, who would make up the rules as they went. With them, you could catch a pass and get excited, thinking, "Touchdown! Yeah!" And the guys who were

---

* James 1:19
† Ephesians 4:29, NLT

making up the rules as they went along would come back and say, "Oh no, no, no! I didn't tell you before, but you're out of bounds." Their made-up rules always left the would-be victor standing there in total shock.

In marriage, we tend to do the same thing. We may laugh at the thought, but often we interact like little kids. We just make the rules up as we go along when handling the issues that arise in marriage. Marital conflict cannot be settled on the fly. It cannot be settled on the cell phone. It cannot be settled in front of the kids at the dinner table. It has to be handled strategically and intentionally.

Effective resolution requires rules of engagement. Having a no-rules, no-holds-barred mode of communication in marriage leaves a lot of open room for conflict, and that's not good because unresolved conflict destroys intimacy. As you and your spouse prepare for the Sexperiment, examine yourselves for ongoing, underlying conflict in your marriage.

It's Time to Unpack Your Baggage

A major source of conflict is baggage brought into the relationship. There are a lot of different bags out there. It could be baggage from previous relationships. There's the baggage that stems from a lack of trust, no matter how justified. There's baggage from past hurts. But a major source of baggage comes from our upbringing.

Lisa and I had dinner a while back with a young couple, and both of them came from families with a lot of baggage. I'll never forget what they told us: "You know, Ed and Lisa, we had no idea of the influence and impact of the baggage that our families gave us." They went on to say how 90 percent of the conflict in their marriage had been because of the family baggage they did not process prior to marriage.

Later, I told Lisa, "They're on to something. This family-baggage thing is the real deal, isn't it?"

Now, let's rewind to when Lisa and I got married. Lisa grew up in a family that was highly, highly organized. For example, when they would go on a family vacation, they would spend months and months planning for it. They would get road maps, highlight the routes, discern how many bathroom stops they would have to make along the way, where they were going to eat, how long they were going to stay at a particular hotel, what the cost would be, and all that stuff. Her dad would even write down all of his stats and figures.

My family? Totally opposite! We'd just jump in the car and start driving for a vacation. We didn't know where we were going to go, where we would end up, or how long we'd be there. We'd just go. So you can probably imagine what happened after Lisa and I got married and took our first vacation. "Let's get ready to rumble!"

If you and your spouse haven't already, it's time to open up your baggage and see what you're carrying around inside. It may seem easier to leave the bag closed and never look in it, but carrying it around is weighing on you. It's weighing down on your marriage because it hinders the communication you need for intimacy.

Whether you intend it to or not, the Sexperiment will open the doors of communication between you and your spouse, perhaps in a whole new way. Out of necessity you start communicating about the quality of your sex life, your hindrances and barriers to intimacy, your need and desire for closeness, and a new way of defining sexual intercourse between husband and wife—as an act of worship.

Proverbs 13:17 (The Message) says, "Irresponsible talk makes a real mess of things, but a reliable reporter is a healing presence." If you want to have marital progress, you need good communication; you need to be a "reliable reporter" with your spouse. If we're going to take marriage to a 'hole 'nutha level, we need to be creative, especially in our communication. What are you doing in your marriage that fosters the kind of atmosphere that leads to creative communication?

The Sweet Science

In my life, I've been blessed to meet a lot of interesting people and have a lot of phenomenal experiences. I've been to countless athletic competitions and sporting events. But several years ago, I witnessed the most exciting event I've ever seen.

I got a call from a friend of mine who said, "Ed, I've got an extra ticket to the world heavyweight championship fight with Mike Tyson if you'd like to go with me." I said, "Are you kidding? Of course I'd like to go!"

So we flew out to Las Vegas and got to witness Iron Mike Tyson fight for the championship of the world. As I sat there watching arguably the greatest boxer to ever live, I couldn't help but be amazed at the strength, power, and skill this man had. He put everything into this fight. He had trained for it, he was prepared for it, and when the time came, he did all he could to execute his plan to win it.

Every marriage will face conflict. Even in the best marriages there will be moments when we go toe-to-toe with our spouse over certain issues. Unlike boxers, we aren't fighting physically. But like Iron Mike, we need to train for these moments so we will know how to handle such situations properly. If couples train together properly to be skilled fighters, they will have marriages that are both successful and succesexful. The biggest component of that training requires creative communication.

Often marital differences end up in all-out combat rather than utilizing creative conflict resolution. Let me give you an example. Some of you grew up in homes where conflict was handled turtle-style. A problem arises, and instead of dealing with the issue, you learned from your family members to retreat into the safety of your shell like a turtle. You don't want to talk about it, so you kind of freeze everyone out. After a while when you think it's safe, you stick your head out of your shell. You take a peek around. The danger has cleared, so you move along on your merry way. The problem with this technique is you become detached and you never deal with the conflict.

Maybe some of you grew up in homes where conflict was handled wasp-style. Wasps are highly aggressive insects. Maybe you saw your parents get into an argument and your father would give your mom those verbal stings right in front of you and your siblings. Then a verbal venom exchange would begin. You grew up thinking that is the way conflict is supposed to be handled, so that is the way you handle conflict today. The problem is, after a while you have an allergic reaction to all the venom and things turn sour.

Marriages end up knocked out on the relational mat with little jabs. It is very rarely a single, giant punch that takes it out. It is the continuous action of those little, tiny digs that wear the marriage down. So we have to get boxer-type training so that our relationships don't sink under the pressure of all those little digs.

Marriages survive and thrive when issues are addressed consistently and in a timely fashion. You need intense training to become champions at managing these marital issues.

Before we can get into what it takes, though, I want to give you a prerequisite: Commit your life to Jesus Christ today, if you haven't already. You cannot understand conflict resolution or reconciliation or how to fight fair until you commit your life to Jesus Christ. Now, I know someone reading this may be thinking, "Come on, Ed. I bought this book to learn how to have a better sex life in my marriage. I wasn't trying to become a Christian." I have to start here, though, because this is the essence of successful conflict resolution.

The apostle Paul said that before Jesus Christ came we were God's enemies.* We can't have peace with others until we have peace with ourselves, and we can't have peace with ourselves until we have peace with God. Once you accept God's son, Jesus, as your savior, you have peace—reconciliation with God.

That reconciliation factor will spill over into every area of

---

* Romans 5:10

your life. You will have the desire to be reconciled with neighbors, co-workers, family members, and especially your spouse.

Our family loves Mexican food. I remember once when the kids were small, after we left a Mexican restaurant Lisa and I laughed that we had four spills in one meal—guacamole, hot sauce, formula, and apple juice. The spills literally touched all of us. That is what happens the moment you know Christ personally. This reconciliation factor spills over into every part of your life.

Committing your life to Christ can change your marriage. But I want to tell you something. The moment you accept Christ into your life, it's not as if your marriage problems will magically vanish. You will have, however, the power to handle anything that comes down the pike.

I have seen marriages that did not have the reconciliation factor in operation and they allowed a minor issue to lead them to divorce. Why? Because instead of having the spirit of reconciliation, they had the spirit of rebellion. On the other hand, I have seen marriages where the reconciliation factor *is* in operation and the couple endures devastating, debilitating problems, yet their marriage comes through it and flourishes even more.

Develop Solution-Driven Conversation

All marriages—poor marriages and unbelievably successful marriages—face the same issues. They all deal with PMS—power, money, and sex! The difference is that great marriages handle conflict in those areas biblically, honestly, openly, truthfully, lovingly, and effectively. What do you and your spouse do the moment conflict arises?

Begin to think in terms of solution-driven conversation. That is tough. It sounds easy, but it's not always. Solution-driven conversation means letting your spouse know that the purpose of the dialogue is not to tear each other apart. It's about coming to a solution about the problem.

The first step in creating solution-driven conversation is *pray about the problem.* Pour out your emotions to God...even your anger. When you get angry, what is the first thing that comes into your mind? Well, I know the first thing that comes into my mind: I am going to straighten Lisa out. She is wrong and I am going to tell her...yada, yada, yada.

You know what the Bible says? Stop and take inventory. Jesus said, in essence, "Don't worry about the speck of sawdust in your spouse's contact lens when you have a sequoia tree in your eye."* He says, "Take the sequoia tree out of your eye before you worry about the speck of sawdust in your spouse's eye." In other words, he's telling us to "yank the plank!"

Here is what I challenge you to do. The moment conflict arises, take a notebook and a Bible and get away for maybe twenty minutes and ask God this question: "God, I really just want to straighten my spouse out right now. I think he (or she) is totally in the wrong. Could I be the one who is being selfish, insensitive, demanding, and critical? Could it be me, God?" Just listen to see what God says to you.

Whenever I have gone away and prayed before attempting to "straighten Lisa out," about 90 percent of the time, guess whose problem it's been? That's right. Mine. When we defer to God, when we allow his spirit to infiltrate us, to work on the interior of our lives, we will understand how to address the inevitable conflicts in marriage.

After you've prayed about it, agree to *negotiate in a neutral setting.* Decide on a neutral setting and come to the negotiating table ready to do some peace talking.

Get at the real issue. Is it money? Is it children? Is it sex? Is it being away too much? Whatever the issue is between you and your spouse, ask God to help you and to give you the creativity to settle the negotiation. It might take you two, three, four, five, six, seven rounds of negotiation, but I promise you, it will serve you well. Before you begin negotiations, make sure you both are rested and have no distractions so you can discuss the situation.

---

* Matthew 7:3–5

Establish Rules of Engagement

Solution-driven dialogue also requires mutually agreed-upon rules of engagement. *Set ground rules* for communication in your marriage. But set them when everything is fine, when you can talk in a rational manner and agree on some principles and precepts that you will abide by when conflict arises.

Colossians 3:8–9 says, "You must rid yourselves of all such things as these..." and the first one is anger. The word *anger* means yelling, volume. Paul also says to get rid of malice. You know what "malice" means? Pushing your spouse's hot button. If you have been married for a while, you know that certain gesture, that little word, or that look that will send your spouse over the edge. That kind of behavior only hinders communication.

Then Paul says, "No insults or obscene talk." That means profane words or derogatory comments must never come from your lips. How can you love and honor in marriage if insults or profanities are being hurled at each other? "Do not lie to each other," he says. Marital intimacy cannot be built on a foundation of lies and dishonesty.

Lisa and I want to share with you some ground rules for engaging in solution-driven conversation. Let me say up front that we do not have all of these covered in our marriage. We are still working on many of these ground rules, even after almost thirty years of marriage. So as we're suggesting, we are also working on this with you.

1. *Never compare*. If conflict arises, never say, "You act just like your mom," or "My father would never do it that way."

2. *Never use absolutes*. "You always..." "You never..." "Every single time..." Absolutes sound like keeping score.

3. *Never fight in the bedroom*. Make love, not war, in the bedroom.

4. *Never threaten your spouse*. Don't use money, sex, or the threat of divorce as leverage to gain the upper hand. Fight fair.

5. *Never change lanes*. You may feel as though you're losing

ground in a particular disagreement, but don't succumb to the temptation to change the subject to another argument to confuse the issue.

6. *Never play reporter*. It's a reporter's job to interrupt people. A reporter will talk with someone and before the person is finished with one answer, the next question is fired off.

7. *Don't play scorekeeper*. "Well, two weeks ago I won and I am going for an undefeated string for the month. I am not going to lose." When you keep score, everyone loses in the relationship.

8. *Don't become a psychologist*. "The reason that you are acting like this is because..." Even if you are a psychologist, no one wants to be analyzed all the time.

9. *Don't play the historian*. The historian looks back into the marital archives and retrieves issues that were going on even in your dating relationship.

10. *Never quit!* Keep believing in God's restoration power in your marriage. Don't give up. Remember the covenant you made before a holy God to love and honor, to cherish, to have and to hold.

A good marriage doesn't have to feel like everything is a bed of roses every moment. Marriage is not going to be that way. There are moments like that, and there should be moments like that. But a lot of it is that day-in, day-out going through the relationship, building it up. It takes huge amounts of raw spiritual courage and guts.

Get FIT with a Personal Trainer

To establish and maintain the kind of intimacy you want to gain through the Sexperiment, you need to get FIT—friendly, intimate, talk. First, talk friendly. Your conversation should be respectful always, no matter how intense the issue being discussed.

Your communication should be not just friendly, but also intimate. That doesn't mean you're always supposed to engage in sexy talk that leads to the bedroom. It means your conversation should be real and honest. In intimate conversation, you allow yourself to be open and vulnerable. You may be amazed at how that openness and vulnerability will lead to the sexual intimacy you desire.

To get FIT, you need the last element of solution-driven conversation—*get a personal trainer*. Proverbs 15:12 (The Message) says, "Know-it-alls don't like being told what to do; they avoid the company of wise men and women."

It's interesting that we ask people's advice for almost everything. You have a legal problem, you talk to an attorney. A financial problem? You might see a CPA. A medical problem? You are going to go to the doctor. A problem with the old golf swing? Hire a golf pro. A problem in your marriage? More often than not we don't say anything to anyone, and certainly not to a professional mediator.

If your marriage is in a rut or if you have gone through nine or ten negotiating-type sessions over the same subject, seek the wise counsel of a Christian couple, preferably one older than you are and who have resolved a similar kind of problem. Make sure this couple knows how to respect your confidentiality. Don't tell your relatives or in-laws, because they're incapable of the kind of neutrality needed to guide you to resolution.

If that still doesn't work, get professional help. Please don't wait too long before addressing the issue. In most marital situations I deal with, the couple has waited too long. They should have come for counseling when the issue surfaced early on.

Don't delay in getting help, because the issue won't simply go away. Go to someone who uses the Bible as the authority. A counselor who maintains biblical authority will know how to guide you to the kind of reconciliation Jesus was talking about.

As a pastor, I believe it is a part of my responsibility to help marriages be fruitful and multiply the way God intended. I want to help my marriage be better. I want to help the couples at Fellowship Church have better marriages. I want to help your marriage too.

For Lisa and me, the whole Sexperiment thing is not a gimmick. It gets a lot of attention, but our sincere desire is to help couples take their masks off, be real, and say, "We really want to stay together, but we need help to do it."

Your marriage is worth making the investment. If you're thinking, "We can't afford professional counseling," think about how great a price you will pay if your marriage doesn't stay together. Your marriage is worth it.

Anytime you have conflict, there is either a breakdown or a breakthrough to a greater level of intimacy. God wants the spirit of reconciliation to move and operate in our lives and in our marriages. God wants all of us to break through into deeper levels of intimacy. That is what He wants. That is what Lisa and I want for our marriage, and we know that is what you want for your marriage. We have the tools, so let's go out and do it!

Action Steps

1. Create a Sexperiment tracking sheet so that you can determine the level and quality of communication in your marriage before, during, and after the challenge. Make notes on how the Sexperiment affects communication in your marriage and share your observations with each other.

2. Read over the communication ground rules with your spouse. If need be, add a few of your own. Acknowledge the ways that you both have violated them in the past. Make an agreement that you will abide by these rules in your marriage, but also agree to make an extra effort to do so during the Sexperiment week.

3. Discuss whether counsel—professional or from a couple you know and respect—is needed in your marriage. If one or both of you are unwilling to go, pray for the willingness to be open and honest about your marital issues with someone you trust.

4. Affirm to each other that you will allow your vulnerability to begin with your communication so that it will extend beyond into the bedroom.

———— *Before You Do* ————

*C*ourtship is an essential part of preparation for marriage. It is a time when you should develop communication, intimacy, spiritual core values, and conflict-resolution. This is important work that must be done during the courtship phase.

Look at the thoughtful ways you communicate now and make a commitment to continue doing so after the ceremony. Please don't assume you no longer need to be cordial and caring after taking your vows. Share with each other the things you like about the way the other communicates. Be honest now about potential communication problems that concern you. Address these matters during premarital counseling.

As you're preparing for marriage, guard yourselves against any temptation to engage in premarital sex so that you do not pole-vault over important issues to get to the electricity of sexual excitement.

Be long-distance runners and pace yourselves according to God's design. God says to spend your prenuptial time working on the hard stuff. Before marriage is the time to work on your communication, not on sex.

Commit to spending a week engaging in communication according to the guidelines suggested in this chapter. Discuss and reflect on how your family has communicated and addressed conflict. What are the values and behaviors you would like to keep? What values and behaviors would you like to avoid duplicating?

As your communication skills grow and develop in the relationship, you will gain confidence in your union and can enter a marriage that will keep sexual intimacy as the beautiful thing God designed it to be.

The Yoke Is Not a Joke

It's important that you connect with the people you date, not just physically, but also spiritually and intellectually. You shouldn't date someone you can't communicate with, no matter how great-looking they are on the outside.

When people date, there's a tendency to assume that because there is an attraction, the other person wants what you want. Not so. Take time to talk...and listen. If the person you're dating communicates poorly or uses foul or crude language, nothing will change if you marry him or her.

If the person buries his or her head in the sand now, that person will do so in marriage. If the person uses anger or aggression to intimidate, the same will happen after the vows. Pay attention now.

As you date, it's also important to look at the other person's family, as people tend to repeat behaviors they grew up with. Observe how the family communicates. What kinds of issues create communication breakdowns? How do they handle conflict?

Does he respect your opinion? Does he value the opinions of women? Does she really listen to you or is she simply agreeing with you to avoid conflict? Those are the important questions to ask and pursue answers to regarding the person you date.

God insists on spiritual compatibility in relationships and on His son driving the car of the person you date, and ultimately marry. God wants us to discover the great destination that He has for all of our lives. He wants us to discover the track He has designed for us. And He has designed an awesome track; after all, He thought it up.

9

Boom Chicka Wah-Wah (and Other Lessons from the R & B Industry)

I've performed a lot of wedding ceremonies. At the conclusion of the ceremony, I look into the starry eyes of the bride and groom and say, "I now pronounce you husband and wife, in the presence of God and these assembled witnesses." Then I add from the Bible, "What God has joined together, let man not separate."*

At this point, everything seems so perfect, so right. The man and the woman have just exchanged vows and rings and kisses. The marriage is for keeps. Right? Well, for a lot people it is. Even after years of marriage, I'm always pleased when couples tell me, "Ed, we have a great marriage. We are more in love today than we were when we walked down the aisle. Marriage is great!"

Conversely, I'm always saddened by the other couples who shrug their shoulders and say, "Well, our marriage is so-so. I'm just doing my time in a prison cell of predictability." It's sad to me that they resign themselves to settle for stale, mundane, and routine in the most powerful human union God ever created.

---

* Matthew 19:6

After a few years of marriage, kids, and in-laws, some couples are in a sort of relational purgatory. They hover somewhere between marital fulfillment and divorce. They tell me, "My marriage is hanging by a thread, Ed. It's in the deep weeds."

All couples go through periods when the marriage feels mundane, like they are stuck in a rut. It happens after prolonged periods of doing the same thing the same way, over and over, yet they wonder why their marriage seems so predictable and mundane. Husbands and wives need creativity in marriage to keep the relationship fresh, unpredictable, and spontaneous, which helps maintain intimacy and sexual excitement.

Keeping those feelings of romance and intimacy alive in your marriage after years requires creativity. Being creative in your marriage could mean getting a new wardrobe for the bedroom or planning a special weekend away just for making love. It might mean infusing the relationship with a little romance (flowers, candlelit dinners, long walks, and talks), like you did when you were dating. It definitely means keeping date night sacred in your marriage (every week or at least twice a month) and thinking of new things to do together to keep the relationship moving forward.

You and your spouse alone on a date is the venue where you draw away, where you're alone. You can share your fears and your dreams and your questions and desires. It's a place and time of vulnerability. That's why I encourage couples to take trips together at least once or twice a year.

Creativity in marriage pays big dividends in the relationship. I'll give you a great example of Lisa's creativity in our marriage. At the time, we had spent more than thirty Valentine's Days together (including dating and marriage). What can you do to be creative after more than three decades of Valentine's Days? Well, Lisa thought of something. She took a picture of us and had it framed with a giant mat around it. When I saw it I wondered, "Why the giant mat? Why not use a bigger picture or a smaller frame?" But it was all part of her plan to make our Valentine's night special and unique.

That night, she put the picture with the giant mat on our bed, along with two Sharpie markers. She said, "Honey, we're going to write about our relationship."

I said, "What?"

She explained further. "We're going to use the mat to write meaningful words about our thirty-one years of being together. I have some things in mind already, and we're writing them on the picture mat."

So we began to write. At first I didn't know what to think because writing those things made me feel vulnerable. But the more I wrote, the more I got into it. Now it is one of my favorite pictures. I have it hanging in my office.

Lisa wrote down memories like "Carport kisses," "Charlie perfume" (the cologne she used to wear), and "Jovan Musk Oil" (my cologne of choice back in the day). One funny one we wrote was "Boo to you, too."

After Lisa and I had been dating for several weeks, and I was over at her house, we were sitting on the couch downstairs watching television and I was thinking, "OK, should I kiss her?"

As I was debating whether I should try to kiss her, she asked, "Would you like something to eat?"

I said yes, so she ran upstairs to get me something to eat. I thought, "OK, I'm going to hide and scare her. Then maybe she'll jump into my arms and plant one on me."

So I ran and hid as I heard footsteps coming down the stairs. As the footsteps stopped, I jumped out from where I was hiding and said, "Boo!"

It was Lisa's mother. And her mom looked at me and said, "Boo to you, too!"

That story is a great memory for us, and that evening was a very special Valentine's Day because of Lisa's special creative effort.

Creativity is different for every couple because, by definition, it is unique to each person or circumstance. The point is to just go for it and be creative within your God-given capacity to shake things up for the better in your marriage.

I won't kid you. Creativity in marriage takes motivation, energy, and effort. If you're not injecting creativity in your relationship, you're probably already feeling the effects of marriage in a rut.

When you and your spouse take on the Sexperiment, you posture yourselves to relate to each other creatively. Through your week of sex, you can employ new ways of being creative both in and out of the bedroom. It's important to be creative both inside and outside the bedroom because the intimacy that happens in bed begins long before you get there.

One of the important ways to shake things up pre-bedroom is through marital communication. Couples should communicate with each other—both verbally and nonverbally—in ways that build intimacy and excitement about making love and being in a relationship with each other. Open and consistent communication helps keep down the barriers that block closeness and enjoyment in marriage.

Barriers to Intimacy

Some married couples can't return to a place of intimacy in their relationship because they've put up too many barriers over the years. In fact, some couples can't even see their way to completing the Sexperiment because of barriers in their marriage. They may say, "A week of sex? No way we can make time for that! We've got too many things going on . . . the kids, the job, the church meetings . . ."

Barriers can be a good thing, like the fences people put up to protect their animals and keep them from running away or into danger. As good as barriers can be for us and as much protection as they can provide, they can also be disastrous. It all depends on what they are, who puts them there, what they keep out (or in), and what we do with them.

We've briefly discussed in other chapters the fact that, over time, married couples tend to erect barriers around their bedroom. Barriers are different from the guardrails we discussed in chapter six. Barriers keep intimacy out while guardrails protect the couple within them.

You may not be able to see the barriers in your marriage as you've erected them, but they exist. The blockades you and your spouse have created within your marriage are the very things that are keeping you from experiencing marriage the way it's meant to be. Those barriers keep you from connecting on a regular basis with your spouse. In short, they keep you from having enough sex.

When you get married, the barriers that block the bedroom aren't that big. It's easy to hop over them with minimal effort. The whole adventure of marriage is so new and fresh and exciting that the few barriers that do exist are just a few inches off the ground. Newlyweds don't mind those early barriers because the payoff equals pleasure!

When Lisa and I got married, we lived in a little apartment in Houston. It was just the two of us. No kids. (We have four now.) No dogs. (We have five now.) No multiple campuses of a church to oversee. (We have five of those now too.) It was easy in the beginning to hop over the barriers to intimacy. Over the years, however, we have learned to keep the barriers down so that our marriage won't be blocked by a lot of stuff, even though we both lead very busy lives.

However, as time ticks on, the barriers in any marriage grow and can easily become some major obstructions. All of a sudden, or at least it seems that way, the effort it takes to overcome the barriers to intimacy seems overwhelming.

And if you aren't careful, pretty soon the barriers can become so cumbersome that you and your spouse would rather avoid dealing with them altogether than engage in the effort it takes to overcome them. The danger is that if the barriers aren't dealt with, they will eventually get so big that the bridge back to marital intimacy can no longer be traversed. The obstacles will appear larger than the payoff. If this goes on long enough, you ultimately may decide to bail rather than do what it takes to break through.

The Sexperiment has been so good and healthy for a number of couples who are stuck on the other side of the bridge to intimacy. It jump-starts the process of getting over, under, or around barriers.

> Thank you, thank you! This [Sexperiment], Ed, is golden! Showers of praise from my wife and I, whose sex life over the years has stagnated and become, I suppose, a little rusty.
>
> We have a ritual now, my wife and I: after dinner, sit by our fire and share a cup of tea, bagging our usual TV indulgences in favor of talking and sharing our days, which leads not only to emotional intimacy but, now with your challenge, a desire to turn that back into physical intimacy as well.
>
> Sanchez

It seems paradoxical that a couple would construct barriers to keep themselves from regularly experiencing the deepest intimacy possible. But it happens to all couples at some point in the marriage.

Let me explain something before going further. These barriers usually aren't bad. Most of the time, they are good things. But too many good things in life can keep you from experiencing the best things in life. This is especially true when it comes to having sex with your spouse. The good things in life outside the bedroom can crowd out the power and passion of married sex inside of it.

These barriers to the bedroom are obstacles you will have to fight the week you participate in the Sexperiment. You may have to slowly begin to change some things in your life in order to complete the week and overcome them for good.

Kids

It may seem ironic how something that sex produces is the very thing that can keep sex from actually happening. But it does. Children can be both a blessing and a blockade in the marriage, both at the same time. Kids can definitely keep you from connecting sexually.

Lisa and I have four children, so this barrier is something that we have had to negotiate time and again for more than twenty years. From the moment we had our first daughter, it was obvious that we were dealing with a serious barrier to the bedroom!

When the marriage becomes too focused on the kids, a barrier begins to grow that turns the place for romance into a sleep station. When parents allow raising kids to be their primary purpose, the focus is no longer on the most important relationship in the family— the marriage. The energy and attention you invest in the children becomes greater than the energy and attention you and your spouse place on each other. And when you finally do have time for sex, you just want to roll over and start counting sheep.

Short-term, for the duration of the Sexperiment, have a plan for how you will handle your child-rearing responsibilities yet still make time to make love. You can do it! Once you do it for a week, you will begin to see ways to restructure your relationship going forward so that your children are blessings, not barriers.

Careers

Every day, millions of people wake up early, take a shower, get dressed, check themselves in the mirror, and head off to the market-place. From auto mechanics to administrative assistants to Fortune 500 CEOs, the mind-set is the same—we go into the world and put our best foot forward to get the biggest reward possible. While there's nothing inherently wrong with that, it can easily become a blockade to connecting with your spouse sexually.

It's not that we intentionally want to move away from our spouse, but when we focus so much of our energy and attention away from the marriage, something gets left behind. And that something is so often the other spouse. When we finally get home from climbing the corporate ladder all day, the only thing we want to do is get comfortable, settle in on the couch, and just unwind.

When you decide to make the Sexperiment a priority for completion, your career must be put into perspective. Plus, if you've been putting your career first, and men often do this, it will give your spouse an extra boost to know that he or she has now taken priority over work. Let your spouse know how important your marriage is by prioritizing time to make love and create a greater depth of intimacy. Then, after you do it for a week you can begin to find ways to put marriage and career in perspective moving forward.

Commitments

Many of us, if we are totally honest with ourselves, would admit that we are overcommitted. In today's fast-paced world, it's easy to recognize that we have a lot going on. Most of the time, we have too much going on. Even our leisure time is overscheduled.

Too often, we want to be all things to all people. We want to join every social club we can because we see the importance of meaningful relationships in our lives. We want to have as much time on the golf course or at the lake as we can, because leisure is an important aspect to a well-rounded life. We want our kids to be in every possible extracurricular activity because we want them to enjoy childhood. We also may even try to shove church into our packed schedule, because we want to cover the spiritual base as well.

Meanwhile, we'd love to connect intimately with our spouse. But when? The kids need to get to soccer practice, we're at the office for sixty hours a week, the next home-improvement project is looming, there's family to visit, BBQs to attend, laundry that needs folding, a yard that needs mowing, and of course we can't miss those shows we recorded on the DVR.

The list of obligations seems endless, but the one that gets left out of the mix is the commitment we made before any of that other stuff was even on the radar—that's the one we made to our spouse when we said "I do."

When was the last time you and your spouse blocked out two to three hours just for each other (no kids, no long day at the office, no run to the grocery store, etc.)? Well, if you're not doing it now, the Sexperiment will lead you in that direction. When you make time for sex with your spouse during that week, you will do some reassessment and reevaluate how important those other things really are. You will discover that your marriage is more important than a golf game or a club committee meeting.

Creativity is fueled by energy. You need energy to be creative, but the result of being overly committed is fatigue. We're too tired to be creative with intimacy and communication. That leaves couples wanting to have more sex, but they just never seem able to get past the barriers. With kids, careers, and commitments all putting up barriers to intimacy in the bedroom, the work it takes to get back to the bedroom seems like too much.

One morning, one of my young daughters looked up at me and asked, "Dad, when you saw Mommy for the first time, did you whistle?" God has given us this wolf-whistle desire for the opposite sex. He has given us the gift of sex and He has provided a valuable venue through which we may practice and utilize this gift—marriage.

But that doesn't mean that the desire or the opportunity comes easily within marriage. We have to work at it. Remember the MWE (marital work ethic) that I mentioned before? To help you as you successfully and creatively complete the Sexperiment with your spouse, and to move beyond with intentional intimacy, Lisa and I have some suggestions we call Sex Builders.

Sex Builders will help you get rid of the things that are keeping you from being the kind of mate, sexually speaking, that God wants you to be. If you want to make love regularly and creatively, pay attention to them.

Sex Builder #1: Know What God Says About Sex

When you don't know or understand what God says about something, let me encourage you to search for the answer. There is a huge link between spirituality and sexuality. Couples who make time to express love to God in an authentic way also make time to make love together frequently and creatively.

I have talked to numerous couples who have Christ-centered marriages. I've found that they overwhelmingly tend to have wonderful, mutually satisfying sexual relationships. Study after study shows that the most sexually satisfied people in marriage are those who pray together, those who read the Bible together, and those who go to church together. God made sex, and they are doing it the way He wants them to do it.

The Bible says, "Let the husband fulfill his duty to his wife and likewise, also, the wife to her husband. The wife does not have authority over her own body, but the husband does. And likewise, also, the husband does not have authority over his own body, but the wife does."* That means your spouse is the manager over your body. You are the manager over your spouse's body.

Sex Builder #2: Dial into Your Spouse's Sex Drive

We've talked about how some couples are clueless about the varying sex drives between men and women. A man's sex drive is kind of like a sprint. In an instant, just like that, he is ready to sprint into sex. A woman's sex drive, on the other hand, is more like a 5K run. She, more or less, jogs into sex.

God has wired us differently with unique sex drives. A husband experiences sex and from his sexual experiences flow his feelings.

---

* 1 Corinthians 7:3, NKJV

The wife is the polar opposite. She has to experience feelings before she can experience physical intimacy.

Here is how things get messed up. The husband, the sprinter, approaches his wife the way he wants to be approached. He is aggressive in taking initiative and he sprints into sex. In turn, the wife approaches her husband the way she wants to be approached, with romance, with intimacy, with gentleness. She jogs into sex.

Wives and husbands who have it together in the intimacy department dial into each other's sex drive. Let me put it this way: For the most part, men desire sex more than their wives do. You could have just been in a major argument five minutes earlier. As a man, you are still likely to pat your wife on the posterior and say, "Hey, hey, hey. How about you and me head to the bedroom?"

Wives, on the other hand, are multifaceted and multidimensional. The context surrounding the sexual part of the relationship is huge for them. Women have to know that everything is OK outside the bedroom before everything gets OK between the sheets.

So what do we do about it? Husbands, quit being a sprinter all the time and jog a little bit with your wife. Wives, don't always run so slowly. Try incorporating some sprints into that 5K run.

When the husband is thinking about her needs and the wife is thinking about his needs, you'll have two people understanding the pace of passion. If you want to get your partner in the mood, approach him or her the way he or she wants to be approached.

Sex Builder #3: See Through the Secular Smoke Screen

The smoke screen of lust distorts the realities of a biblical commitment in marriage. Run your love life through the scriptural grid and see what the Bible says about one man and one woman committed to God and to each other in the context of marriage—a man and woman who are selflessly serving each other with energy and creativity.

These couples see sex as an opportunity for greater intimacy and mutual discipleship. In short, it's a win-win for these couples.

After speaking on this subject in one of our weekend worship services at Fellowship Church, one lady commented enthusiastically to Lisa, "I really enjoyed today's message. My husband and I are going to go home and do some discipleship."

Sex Builder #4: Take Care of the Temple

This Sex Builder comes from the Bible: "Do you not know that your body is the temple of the Holy Spirit, who is in you, whom you have received from God?"* Take care of the temple. If you are a Christ follower, your body is a temple, the dwelling place of God's Spirit.

Don't trash your temple. I am not talking about turning into a Ken and Barbie couple or developing a physical obsession that can take over your life. I am saying, though, to do the best with what you have. Eating properly, exercising, and staying as fit as possible are acts of worship to God. The apostle Paul says, "Offer your bodies as living sacrifices, holy and pleasing to God."†

It takes a commitment of hard work to continue to court your spouse by maintaining your physical appearance. Don't neglect the obvious: You can't keep your sex life in shape if you don't keep your body in shape. When we take care of our body, our temple, we are expressing love to God and love for our spouse.

Sex Builder #5: Stop Depriving Each Other

Make love, not excuses. Those aren't my words; they're from God. Back in biblical times, some people were having arguments about

---

* 1 Corinthians 6:19, NKJV
† Romans 12:1

what to do when one spouse was in the mood and the other not. The apostle Paul, inspired by the Holy Spirit, told them, "Stop depriving one another except by an agreement for a time, so that you may devote yourselves to prayer."* Aside from certain medical problems or health issues, the only excuse we should give is "I'm in prayer." But you must both be in agreement about this.

I don't think the Bible is telling us that we can't ever say no. But no should be the exception. And don't just say no. If you say no, say no with an appointment, like, "No, tomorrow night." This appointment gives the two of you something to look forward to.

A big excuse these days is "I'm tired." But being fatigued for the most part is a mental thing. I love fishing; especially fly-fishing in salt water. When I'm on a fishing trip, I can get up at four a.m., ready to fly-fish. I might be physically tired, but mentally I'm ready to fly-fish for tarpon. And that mental attitude helps perk up my tired body.

Too tired for sex? Mentally tell yourself, "I am having sexual intercourse with my husband, with my wife, my covenant partner. Mentally, I am going to say I am ready." You'll be amazed how your body will follow this mental commitment.

It takes two to tango. If you want a great marriage with creativity and newness, you both had better be involved. If you want great romance, you had better both be taking part. If you want great sex, you had better both be aroused—mentally and physically.

Sex Builder #6: Take a Romantic Getaway

This Sex Builder is to get on board the B-52. B stands for a break, and 52 stands for fifty-two weeks out of the year. Husbands and wives, I challenge you to take two breaks a year just for the two of you—no kids, no in-laws, not even another couple. Go away a night or two twice a year, every six months. Go away to fan the flames of your

---

* 1 Corinthians 7:5, NASB

romance. Go away for intimacy. Go away for sex. In fact, you can begin your Sexperiment with a weekend getaway.

If you're thinking about all the reasons why you can't pull off a romantic getaway, I challenge you to use creativity to make it happen. It is better to pay the price now, take out a loan if you have to, than to end up relationally bankrupt later on down the road. Taking these breaks is worth it, and you will reap huge benefits in your marriage.

Sex Builder #7: Discuss Sex Openly with Your Spouse

Sit down and share your likes and dislikes, wants and desires, problems and needs. Put it on the table and deal with it. Use your week of the Sexperiment to determine areas of your sex life that have been neglected.

If you're uncomfortable talking about sexual matters, then start slowly until you can develop a mutual comfort level for heart-to-heart sharing. The greatest thing in sex is communication, so please find a way to bring communication into the marriage bed.

Sex Builder #8: Bring Back the Romance

God's design for marriage is that we be monogamous, not monotonous. Marriage becomes monotonous when there is no creativity. The relationship becomes stale and rut-like—same old look, same old conversation, same old lovemaking.

Instead of monotony, we need to model our lives and relationships after the essence of God, who is highly creative and innovative. If we know God and live for Him and worship Him corporately and individually, we are going to have creativity in every area of our lives. You can't do the same things the same way and expect unique results. We have to change. We have to work. We have to kick monotony out and let sex be the pleasurable gift that God wants it to be.

If you look up the word *impractical* in the thesaurus, one of the synonyms is *romantic*. We have to become impractical people of romance, like Solomon and his wife. They were creative in their communication and in their lovemaking.

Solomon was creative. He made his wife earrings; he wrote poetry for her. He even paneled the master bedroom by himself with fine wood cut from the cedars of Lebanon. He took her on long walks through the forest.

His wife responded to his creativity the way he wanted to be approached because he had approached her the way she wanted to be approached. The Bible says that she danced before him in a sheer negligee.* It says that Solomon took her to a biblical B&B. Solomon's wife took the initiative and said to him, "Solomon, let's make love outdoors. I want to show you something old and something new."

It is our prayer that you and your spouse will enjoy sex within God's parameters and use this amazing gift the way He desires. Thank God for that wolf-whistle desire for the opposite sex. Let's build great sex into our marriage by using these Sex Builders and eliminating the sex busters. Have fun!

Action Steps

1. Get creative! As you prepare for your Sexperiment week, get your creative thinking cap on. Think about your spouse. Consider his/her sexual wants and likes and how you can creatively meet them.

2. Plan a simple romantic gesture for each day of the Sexperiment (for example, a single rose on the bed, cooking breakfast for

---

* Song of Solomon 6

your spouse, putting a love note in a place he or she will see it after you've gone to work, calling during the day to say "I love you").

3. Be honest about the barriers that block intimacy in your marriage. Determine those that you have the power to remove right away, and do so. Discuss those barriers with your spouse so you both can figure out creative ways to eliminate them and make time for intimacy.

4. Schedule at least two date nights. The first one should kick off your Sexperiment week, if possible. Commit to honoring those dates as if they are the most important appointments of your life.

——— *Before You Do* ———

*G*etting to know each other can be fun and exhilarating. And it's important to get to know each other apart from physical intimacy. Why? Sex is so powerful that it can blind your reasoning abilities. It can cause you to bypass critical areas of relationships because you're focused on sex. Then, only after you are married do you discover how important those previously neglected areas are to intimacy.

I have a close friend who lives on the West Coast. He was a college athlete and, during that time, he was very promiscuous. He became a Christian later on and got married. After several years, his marriage was going through a lot of struggles and was hanging by a thread. He was getting ready to do something that was so stupid that I could not believe it. But by the grace of God and some honest confrontations from his Christian friends, he and his wife sought Christian counseling.

Thankfully, they got back on track and are now doing great. But he would be the first to tell you that the reason he had those issues in marriage was because he was so promiscuous before marriage. He essentially had brought all of those other women into the bedroom with his wife.

During your time of engagement, don't do anything that will bring other people or variables into your marriage that may cause you great trouble or heartache later.

——— *The Yoke Is Not a Joke* ———

*R*omance is a wonderful thing! There's nothing like the sultry lyrics of a love song to stir our desire for intimacy. Romance, love songs, and going the extra mile for someone you love are all wonderful ways to show how much you care. As a single person, always be aware that these actions should lead to intimacy in marriage.

Sitting with someone you care for and listening to romantic songs or watching romantic movies can cause you to wish for that kind of relationship in your own life—and you can have it. But please make up your mind to have it God's way. If you've been disciplined enough to keep yourself from premarital sex, don't give up. I know it's hard; the temptation can seem unbearable at times, but God will reward you for your faithfulness. Do whatever it takes to preserve this sacred act and reserve it for marriage.

Don't fall into the seductive lure of romantic words and feelings. Be on your guard. Don't deceive yourself by saying, "Oh, I can handle it. I'm not going to give in to these urges." God knows how hard this area is for us, so He warns us to get out when the fire starts to get too hot. Instead, find ways to be romantic without being sexually suggestive. Use your creativity to show someone that he/she is special to you without throwing yourselves into temptation.

10

The Real Big "O"

I remember the first time I saw a high-definition television. They were pretty expensive back then, but the difference between the high-definition television and the set that I was watching at home was just amazing. It was television on a 'hole 'nutha level.

God has a high-definition image of the covenant union between a husband and wife; it's marriage on a 'hole 'nutha level.

Comparing God's high-definition marriage to a typical marriage is like comparing high-definition television to analog television. As you get closer to God's definition of marriage, the picture becomes brighter, clearer, and more vivid. On the other hand, as you look at marriage from the way that society thinks, it gets more blurry as you get closer to it. You can see the lines and pixels and the snow and everything, like on an old tube-style television.

Through the Sexperiment, you and your spouse will be set on course for marriage in HD. What does it mean to have a marriage in HD? Obviously it takes more than a week of sex, but those seven days can be an amazing preview of what HDM—high-definition marriage—is all about.

By devoting yourselves to sexual intimacy with each other for an entire week, you will work together cooperatively to make it happen with creativity and excitement, prioritizing and rearranging schedules. Couples committing to and completing a week of sex is oneness in action.

God designed marriage to be lived in high definition, and we can. Our lovemaking, our parenting, and even our conflict resolution should be in HD. As you look closer into a high-definition marriage, you get a better, clearer picture of some critical aspects of marriage.

First of all, in HD marriage you are going to see some high-definition unconditional love—HD love. Our culture upholds marriage built on conditional love in a 50/50 partnership approach. We say, "If you do A-B-C and 1-2-3, then I'll love you." Or, "If you keep your half of the bargain, then I'll keep mine."

But that's not the kind of love the Bible tells us to have toward each other. The Bible teaches that spouses are to have *unconditional* love toward each other. That's love on another level, a higher definition.

Unconditional love plays itself out in the Sexperiment when one spouse is displeased about something the other spouse did, but does not withhold sex, because both agreed to the seven-day challenge. That same unconditional love you engage in in order to complete the Sexperiment is the same kind of love you should employ every day, in every area of your marriage, including sex.

The Bible teaches that there are several levels of love. The first level is *agape,* or covenant love. It's the initiative-taking love that Jesus has for you and me. It's the love that moved him to go to the cross and die for our sins, even though he was without sin. His unconditional love means there is nothing I can do that will cause Jesus to love me less.

A while back a friend of mine was in the process of building a pretty amazing house. He took me on a tour. The design work, the rooms, the flow of the house, and the view were all something to behold, but the house was being built in a part of the Dallas Metroplex that has some pretty bad soil. So I asked him about the foundation.

"How long did you work on the foundation?" I asked. His reply shocked me.

He told me he spent about six months just on the foundation. Six months! After I saw how large the house was going to be, he *needed* to spend six months working on a solid foundation.

This is the key to high-definition marriage. We've got to have a well-built foundation of covenant love.

The House That Love Builds

The Sexperiment is your starting point to building or reevaluating the foundation of your marriage. Having sex for seven days may not be convenient for you, but because you are in a covenant relationship, you submit to the sexual needs of your spouse.

Unconditional love—*agape* in marriage—means dying to self and giving yourself to your spouse without reservation.

Another level of covenant love mentioned in the Bible is *phileo*. This kind of love represents connectivity. It's the warm and fuzzy side of love. It's the motivation for companionship that draws out of covenant love. We've got to have *agape* as the foundation, but we also need to have *phileo* to connect with each other.

You and your spouse will connect in *phileo* as you spend time together, simply because you enjoy each other's company. You connect in *phileo* as you show your spouse thoughtfulness and kindness.

Obviously, you can't just jump into bed every day for seven days during your Sexperiment week, and this is especially true for women. Remember, husbands, women are long-distance runners or joggers when it comes to sex. Intentionally showing *phileo* toward each other during the Sexperiment can help you begin the habit of demonstrating thoughtfulness to each other and take your oneness to a deeper level, both in and out of the bedroom.

Finally, there's another kind of love that almost seems like a popular obsession these days, and the Bible mentions this one as well—

eros. We get the word *erotic* from it. That's the steamy, passionate, sexual side of love.

Think of your marriage like a house that has *agape* as its foundation and is built up on its sides with *phileo* and *eros*. So we've got *agape*, we've got *phileo*, and we've got *eros*. But the dwelling is still in jeopardy because something is still missing—a covering.

What happens if a house is built without a roof? The house will have no protection from the elements. Even though it is built on a solid foundation, and is fortified on its sides by kindness (*phileo*) and passion (*eros*), if it starts to rain, everything inside would be destroyed.

It has to have a roof. The kind of love that most closely parallels to having a roof on your house is a biblical term God uses when He talks about a covenant—*hesid*. I like the word *hesid* because the letter *h* is on one end and *d* is on the other—the anchor points for marriage in HD.

Hesid is God's tenacious love, the loyal love that God has for His children.

God says throughout the Bible that marriage should mirror His love for His people. Once we are under the authority of God's high-definition marriage, we will be inspired to do positive things we normally wouldn't do. We will say things we normally wouldn't say.

The apostle Paul says that marriage is mysterious.* I believe the word *mysterious* refers to covenant love, because people in the secular world don't get it.

Maybe you're thinking, "Well, Ed, the world says that love is accidental, 'a secondhand emotion.' Love is just uncontrollable."

That is not real love. The Bible talks about real love as authentic love. And that kind of love is a decision, a choice.†

Every morning I get up and put on clothes. I don't just blindly reach into my closet and pull out a shirt and a pair of slacks. Every morning I make a decision about what to wear. I make a choice to get dressed and to color coordinate.

---

* Ephesians 5:32
† Colossians 3:14

In the same way we have to make the decision to put on love each day.

I've officiated a lot of weddings in my life. Every time I say to the groom, "Do you choose to take this bride?"

To the bride I've said, "Do you choose to take this husband?" I ask, "Do you *choose*" because love is a choice.

I don't say, "Well, do you *feel* like loving your wife like Christ loved the church?" Neither do I ask, "Do you feel like loving him, even when he does something just totally dumb?"

God knows us better than we know ourselves. He knows that a high-definition marriage, which is marital oneness taken to its highest level, cannot be based on feelings, because feelings get freaky. God knows marriages can't be based on lust, because lust has lapses. He knows marriage cannot be based on looks, because looks can get lost after a while.

Covenant marriage cannot be based on circumstances, because circumstances change. That's why God has said, over and over again, that marriage must be based on covenant love—*agape* and *hesid*—because love is a decision.

Love is also a behavior. Jesus said, "If you love me, you will obey what I command."* In other words, you're going to *do* the stuff. Christ basically said, "If you love me, you're going to show me that you love me by the fruit you produce, by what you say, by what you do, and by the activities you engage in."

Love also is commitment. Jonathan Cude is a Christian psychotherapist who attends Fellowship Church. He said to me one time, "Marriage must be built on the cold steel of commitment." That's *agape*.

In the nearly thirty years of my marriage, there have been some moments when I have not felt wonderful, romantic feelings for Lisa—not 24/7, anyway. But we have based our marriage on *agape* and *hesid*. And because we base it on that kind of love, the other types of love follow, even though they fade from time to time.

---

* John 14:15

When you choose to practice *agape* and *hesid* in your marriage, the other forms of love remain, even when they're being actively expressed. You will not experience an electrical charge for your spouse every day of your marriage, so you can't base your marriage on feelings. God knows how fickle our feelings can be, so He designed HD marriage to be built on high-definition covenant love.

When people got into covenants with each other in the Old Testament, as I discussed in earlier chapters, they would make pledges to each other and to a witnessing public. They would rededicate themselves to this commitment, and that's what we need to do in our marriages.

Use your Sexperiment week to recommit to each other, and the feelings of love will flow. Begin to get under the influence of high-definition marriage and high-definition love.

If you build your marriage on *agape*, start yielding yourself to those things that are the hard, cold steel of commitment. I promise you that the *phileo* and *eros* stuff will flow behind them like a river following along a natural path.

It's easier to act our way into feelings than to feel our way into actions. Remember, feelings get funky, so we've got to base it on something higher, on something bigger and bolder. The Sexperiment is the starting point for you and your spouse to say to yourselves, "We're going to build a high-definition marriage."

The Bible says, "Unless the Lord builds the house, its builders labor in vain."* That's the problem with marriages that are not built on covenant love. The husbands and wives are simply builders laboring in vain because they don't understand what marriage is all about.

You're not going to find the answer to a higher level of oneness in marriage through psychobabble or the media. You're not going to find the answer through movies, sitcoms, reality television shows, or romance novels.

When you get up close to high-definition marriage, you always

---

* Psalm 127:1

see high-definition, unconditional love. It's not about you; it's about your spouse.

ForGIVEness Bears the Load

Unconditional love is the foundation of high-definition marriage. *Phileo* and *eros* are the walls that provide security and shielding from outside elements. And all of this works well most of the time. Couples enjoy feelings of erotic love and warm fuzzies grounded in unconditional love.

But then a crisis happens or issues arise and put pressure on the relationship. It may threaten the entire home, right down to the foundation. That's where the load-bearing walls of the house become ultra-important. Forgiveness is the load-bearing wall of the house.

In construction, depending on the type of building and the number of stories, load-bearing walls are put in place to carry the weight of the dwelling. Without load-bearing walls, an outer wall could become unstable if the load exceeds the strength of the material used. That could cause the entire structure to collapse to its foundation.

A foundation of love keeps the relationship strong. That is the place on which the relationship stands. But forgiveness in a relationship is the barometer of oneness. Forgiveness bears the load and allows the house to stand and keep standing, even when it is shaken. A lot of marriages collapse because they did not make use of their load-bearing wall of forgiveness.

Marriage in HD must have forgiveness in HD. You can have all the love, the feelings, the desire, but unforgiveness will cause your house to collapse. Many couples divorce despite still liking each other and maybe even still being in love. Why? Because they did not have high-definition, unconditional love and would not let forgiveness bear the load in their marriage.

When you have high-definition, unconditional love, it always segues into high-definition forgiveness, which is the essence of the covenant.

Right in the middle of forgiveness is the word *give*. The Bible says, "Be kind and compassionate to one another, forgiving each other, just as in Christ God forgave you."*

Taking oneness to another level is about forGIVEness. You and your spouse can't come closer together if you have issues blocking your intimacy because of unforgiveness. Ask your spouse for forgiveness so that you can come together sexually. ForGIVE your spouse so that you can come together sexually.

A lot of spouses are blocked because they need to give or receive forgiveness. A lot of spouses need to confess, "I was wrong. I'm sorry. Will you forgive me?" It's that simple to say.

Asking for forgiveness isn't always easy; neither is extending it to someone who has wronged you. But you cannot let it hold you back from that higher level of oneness. Forgiveness will lift a burden off of your shoulders, it will reconnect the relationship, and it will bring you closer to the character of Christ. It will also move your marriage into a deeper level of intimacy.

High-definition love and oneness taken to a new level call for a higher definition of forgiveness. The apostle Paul says, "Bear with each other and forgive whatever grievances you may have against one another. Forgive as the Lord forgave you."†

Jesus told a story about a king who had a lot of money and he loaned the equivalent of $10 million to a guy who worked for him.‡ There was a predetermined time when this guy was supposed to pay the king back the money. Well, at the appointed time, the guy did not have the money and the king was going to throw him to the torturers. But the guy begged for mercy saying, "King, have mercy on me. Give me an extension, please."

And the king said, "OK, I'll give you an extension." Well, the extension came and went and the guy still didn't have the money.

---

* Ephesians 4:32
† Colossians 3:13
‡ Matthew 18:23–35

Do you know what the king did? He said, "I'll forgive you the debt. Don't worry about it." He forgave the guy's $10 million debt!

Now, put yourself in the forgiven man's Nikes. If I had been in his sandals, I would be like, "Wow, this is incredible! I've been forgiven a $10 million debt! I would forgive anybody who ever owed me anything." But here's what happened.

The forgiven man went out and found a guy who owed him something like $17. He started choking the man because he hadn't paid money he owed. The king heard about it and threw the forgiven man to the torturers. Jesus concluded the story by saying, "This is how my heavenly Father will treat each of you unless you forgive your brother from your heart."

Husbands and wives desperately need to be under the influence of high-definition forgiveness because it carries with it another essential tool for marriage—high-definition unselfishness.

That four-letter word, S-E-L-F, is one that I have the most trouble with. Let's just be bold and honest. Selfishness causes most of the conflict we experience in marriage.

The sin of selfishness is messing up our marriages. People say, "Well, I'm not happy. I know God wants me to be happy, so I'm just going to go and find somebody who will make me happy."

Your marriage is not about you; it's about the spouse with whom you are in covenant. The power of covenant love helps us to put "self" in check. There is no way we can contain "self" on our own.

Pray About It

I'm sure you've read all of this stuff and you're thinking, "There is no way I can do all of this, Ed. I can't love unconditionally. I can have *agape, phileo, eros,* and *hesid* all at the same time. This forgiveness stuff is just too hard."

For others of you, the issue may be unselfishness. "I've got to think about me. I can't and I won't lose myself in this marriage. I need to maintain my identity, my personhood." The enemy tricks us into using certain psychobabble to maintain a level of distrust and separateness in marriage.

Marriage is a process of becoming one, but human beings, by nature, are selfish creatures. The need to maintain individuality and a sense of self will very often come into conflict with the covenant call of marriage to become one.

So, how can this be overcome? It certainly is not something that comes naturally to us. We have to pray and ask God to give us the kind of unselfish spirit that will build oneness in marriage. Sound too simple? Prayer is real and it works.

One Sunday night after I preached the Sunday evening worship service at our church in Miami, I went out to eat with some friends there. One of our twins, Landra, had gone with me.

After we had finished eating, the waiter put the bill on the table and my friend picked up the tab. I had my wallet out and Landra looked at it and said, "Dad these credit cards are pretty."

I said, "Yeah, yeah, they are, they are. Now, let me have my wallet back." So, I took the wallet and just put it on my chair under my leg. I thought we were getting ready to go, but we began to talk more and more about Miami and the church.

I could tell Landra was tired, and since I had spoken five times that weekend, I was getting kind of tired too. So I said, "Let's go."

We left the restaurant, jumped into my friend's car, and headed back for the hotel. As Landra and I were going to our rooms, I said, "Landra, do you have my wallet?"

"No."

"Landra, come on, are you kidding me?"

"No."

"Oh no! I have lost my wallet. I'm in Miami and it's gone!"

I picked the cell phone up and called my friend. "Hey, listen," I said. "I know you're close to the restaurant. Would you mind going there and asking our waiter about the wallet?"

So my friend went to the restaurant and talked to the manager, the waiter, and the busboy. Nothing. I rushed down to the lobby and called the restaurant. Nothing. My friend even asked the people who were sitting at the table where we had been to stand up and look around. He looked everywhere.

I was thinking, "This is the worst!" We were looking everywhere.

In the midst of all of my panic, twelve-year-old Landra asked, "Dad, have you prayed about it?"

"No, Landra. The wallet is gone. We're in Miami. The wallet is history. I have not prayed about it."

Suddenly, I felt so convicted. "OK, Landra, I will pray for it," I said.

So we got into a little circle—Landra, several others, and I. I prayed the most pitiful prayer. It was something like: "Dear Heavenly Father, bring me back my wallet. In Jesus's name. Amen." I threw my hands down.

Fifteen seconds later, my cell phone rings, "Mr. Young, we found your wallet."

"What?"

We jumped into the car and drove to the restaurant and picked up my wallet. Someone had been sitting on it. It was the same color as the seat, so when they'd gotten up to look, no one could see it.

Thankfully, nothing was missing from the wallet. All the money was there; all the credit cards were there. When I prayed, God heard me and answered. The prayer was not fancy or elaborate. He didn't just answer me because I'm a preacher who knows a lot of church talk. God is listening to you, too.

I was so excited when I got my wallet back. There is nothing like getting back something that you thought was lost and gone.

Maybe that's true with your marriage. Maybe you're thinking, "OK, my marriage is gone. It's lost. There's no way I can find it again. It's impossible."

If you're feeling that way, then I want to ask you the same question my daughter asked me: "Have you prayed about it?"

Finding What You Lost in Marriage

As you and your spouse work together and pray, God will restore what you've lost in your marriage. He can restore joy. He can restore peace. He can restore desire. He can restore oneness.

When people feel like their marriage is lost, what they have actually lost is a sense of oneness. As selfishness takes over and spouses do things that hurt the other, the oneness leaves and the unforgiveness and hurt take over. Gone is that feeling of "you and me against the world." The special closeness that God desires for a husband and wife to establish diminishes.

When that happens, the walls of *eros* (desire) and *phileo* (warm fuzzies) come tumbling down. *Hesid* caves in on the dwelling, and the structure of your marriage collapses. Only the load-bearing wall of forgiveness can save you and your marriage. It's so important to pray for the willingness and the strength to forGIVE.

Often we pray hoping that God will do something to change our spouse. But so many spouses can tell you that through prayer God didn't change their spouse; He changed them. And when they changed, something in their spouse eventually changed too.

Maybe you're not too excited about praying right now because you want God to change things as you think they need changing. God is all-powerful and all-knowing. He doesn't necessarily work the way we think He should.

But if your goal is to build your marriage and restore oneness, pray anyway, and leave the details to God. Trust Him to know what is best for your marriage. After all, He designed it. Allow Him to do what is needed to build and restore oneness in your marriage.

The very first mention of marriage in the Bible defines oneness as the nature and goal of the marital relationship. It is to become one flesh. The original Big "O" was Oneness, and it still should be.

Sex is a huge part of that. Sexual intimacy between husbands and wives cements the one-flesh relationship so it will last. It will be a testament to our children and a legacy for our culture.

Marriage—which includes sex between a husband and wife—is sacred, because it first and foremost reflects the nature of God. It represents the masculine and feminine characteristics of God coming together as one in those special beings He created in His image.

Seven Days to Oneness

Lisa and I would never try to make you believe that you will achieve a total sense of oneness in your marriage after a week of sex. The objective of this seven-day Sexperiment is to move the marriage relationship to exciting new levels of becoming one: in flesh, in spirit, and in mind.

Sexual intimacy within the boundaries of marriage upholds God's ideal and it enhances our ability to connect with our spouse in a holistic and lasting way. When we commit to keeping the marriage bed a sacred priority, we can move the holy union of marriage to the next level of oneness and beyond.

When married couples commit to take this sex challenge, they experience more than a few moments of excitement and pleasure during a week. They discover that meeting together at the intersection of God and sex can lead them down a life path punctuated by exclamation marks!

As you engage in your seven days to oneness through the Sexperiment, consider the long-range implications of lovemaking in marriage.

Seven things happen when husbands and wives make love and fulfill each other's sexual desires. You and your spouse should review all seven of them during your Sexperiment challenge week. Some of these have been discussed in other chapters, but this synopsis will remind you why God made sex for married couples.

Now, the first thing that happens when we make love in marriage is we fulfill God's purpose for our marriage. Sex is God's gift to married couples to seal the bond of our relationship. During your first day of the Sexperiment, talk with your spouse about God's plan for marriage and how sex plays a pivotal role in the marriage union, especially yours.

The second thing that we do through sexual intimacy in marriage is we reveal our true self. Marriage is a mirror. When we look at our spouse, we see the best and worst of ourselves through them.

Your marriage is a mirror of you, and your sexual intimacy is a mirror of your marriage. It is a reflection of your closeness as a couple. A sexless marriage is headed for trouble. Have you ever avoided the oneness that comes through sexual intimacy?

By participating in the Sexperiment you will, of necessity, take a closer look at the issues in your own life and work to address them so you can move past issues and get on to intimacy. Taking the challenge will get you naked—both physically and emotionally.

The third thing that the Sexperiment brings to marriage is that it helps couples recognize sexual intimacy as a tool for them to thwart sexual temptation. When we have great, fulfilling sex in marriage, we put a barrier of protection around our family and an alarm system around our relationship so that the temptation of outside forces—pornography, lust, extramarital affairs—can be defused. When you have great sex with your spouse, you grow in oneness because you recognize that sex is a sacred act reserved for the two of you.

The fourth effect of the Sexperiment is bringing couples to a conscious awareness of the legacy they leave through marriage. How can we make a difference for the next generation?

Lisa and I are confident that great sex in marriage is a huge part of building a legacy for our children. In our relationship, sexual intimacy gives way to our forgiveness for each other, which gives way to our communication skills and all the other things that matter in marriage.

Our children see those things modeled in their parents' marriage. Now, they don't see the sacredness of our bedroom, but they know that we have that intimacy because it is reflected in all those areas outside the bedroom. So when they choose a spouse, they're going to be thinking deeply about that relationship and what it means and what it stands for. They will have a benchmark by which to measure the romance, the creativity, the love and the spiritual leadership that they should seek in marriage.

The fifth aspect that the Sexperiment highlights is something that you don't really think about when you're having sex. Having sex with your spouse for seven days puts emphasis on the real "F" word—*forgiveness*—and postures you to be kind to one another, as the Bible advises us to do.*

When you and your spouse are making love regularly, intentionally, creatively, and lovingly, there's no getting around forgiveness. You have to deal with the issues and put them aside so that you can continue the physical intimacy. Make forgiveness your friend. Don't let bitterness become an attachment to your spirit.

Lisa really surprised me one day by sharing with me that she tends to hold on to bitterness. But it's something she's aware of and something that she constantly monitors in herself. But it's not just Lisa; we all have to monitor resentment and bitterness that can build up inside of us.

It's important to see resentment for what it is and then be willing to move past it. If you've been married for a while, you already know that there will be times when you don't have every little thing settled before you go to bed. When that happens, what's more important than the unresolved issue is your commitment to each other.

When you said "I do," you weren't making a conditional commitment that says, "Well, not tonight because we haven't settled every issue." If that were the case, most couples would rarely make love.

It's so important to recognize the destructive power of a spouse's refusal to be governed by the unconditional commitment of covenant marriage. If a wife regularly refuses sex because she's holding

---

* Ephesians 4:32

resentment against her husband, sooner or later he will start feeling deprived, and perhaps resentful himself. That's when that attractive co-worker or neighbor, who never seems resentful, starts looking really great to him. The reverse is also true.

Unforgiveness is a breeding ground for adultery. Your relationship does not have to be in perfect harmony in order for you to make love. In fact, most of the time it won't be. Keep working at forgiveness in your marriage because every marriage deals with the same kinds of issues, but the successful marriages negotiate around those barriers and deal with them.

The sixth thing that regular lovemaking demands, as the Sexperiment will demonstrate, is unselfishness. Marriage is all about unselfishness.

When Lisa and I have problems in our marriage, and believe me we do, most of the time it's because I am not seeking God and listening to Him. Problems arise when I've kicked Him out of the Oval Office of my life and decide that I'm running the show.

Evelyn Christenson wrote a book more than thirty years ago titled *Lord, Change Me.** It's a great title and a great way for us to think about marriage. So often I want to tell God, "Lisa is not doing this, and now she's doing that." But the bottom line is that I have to change before God can change things, as I defer and let Him do the rest.

It is easy to look at our spouse's faults and see what is wrong with him or her and not pay attention to self. Lisa and I keep selfishness in check by putting each other's needs above our own. But honestly, the point system gets in the way of that kind of selflessness.

All couples have to fight against the temptation to use the point system in their marriage. It's the system in your head that tells you, "Well, she only gave forty percent so I'll only give forty percent."

That is not what Jesus Christ did for us; He gave 100 percent of himself, and marriage is a reflection of Christ's love for the church. Christ loved the church so much that he gave himself for it. We

---

* Victor Books, 1977

should have that depth of sacrificial love for each other and give 100 percent, even when our spouse is only giving 20 percent.

Giving 100 percent to the marriage is not based on what your spouse does. Covenant marriage is all about fulfilling each other's needs and serving the needs of the other. Even when the points don't look that even across your mental scoreboard, I challenge you to keep on making love.

Fulfilling each other's needs is vitally important in the bedroom. Even during the Sexperiment you may find that one spouse is in the mood and the other is not. Just keep in mind that if you must say "Not now," say it with an appointment.

Once when Lisa and I were doing the Sexperiment, I was exhausted after a long, hectic day, so I told Lisa, "Not tonight, I'm tired. Tomorrow let's double up."

Lisa has helped me understand that women just don't feel the sexual urge all the time like we men tend to do. Her thing is, though, even when you don't feel like it, you can act your way into a feeling rather than feeling your way into an action.

The Bible encourages us to be sensitive to our spouse's needs and not deprive the other sexually.* Lisa and I have seen that one verse revolutionize so many marriages over the years. When spouses do not deprive each other sexually, Satan cannot wedge his way between them with lust.

It has been incredible for spouses to understand that when we love each other like the Lord wants us to, we realize that it's about our spouse. It's not about me. It's not about exhaustion. It's not about being overly committed in my appointments. It is not about the career or my kids. For me, it's about Lisa.

Your relationship with your spouse is what's most important. With that understanding of marriage, you will have the kind of fulfilling and engaging sex life that goes with it. Sexual fulfillment transcends every single area of marriage—and that is true oneness. In action.

---

* 1 Corinthians 7:5

The final thing that we see through the Sexperiment is that it cultivates creativity. Seven straight days of sex could be monotonous, and sex after years or decades of marriage can seem monotonous.

Remember that taking the challenge is not just about completing a task. The Sexperiment has a deeper meaning—loving each other in a more significant way and a more creative way. The seven-day challenge has helped us think more creatively about romance and how to spice up our love life.

Romance and creativity go hand in hand. Think outside the box, not outside the bed. Because when you go outside the marriage bed to be intimate with someone else or to lust after porn models, you've slammed the door to creativity and possibility.

Creativity is just a product of our thought. So we have to be intentional about the desire and need to be creative, and that becomes another way to bring us into oneness.

If you need a little help in the creativity department, take your cues from the Song of Solomon (or Song of Songs) in the Bible. This husband and wife took creativity in romance to the ultimate level.

Sometimes kids make it hard to be creative. Remember, I explained that "kids" is really an acronym for Keeping Intimacy at a Distance Successfully. And they do. When you have kids, you have to be even more creative to have a regular, intentional sex life in marriage.

When our kids were very young, we would feed them first and put them to bed. Then we would have a picnic in our room with candlelight. That was using romance and creativity in the midst of our rather hectic circumstances back then.

After your kids get to be teenagers, though, getting private time to make love won't even be a problem. All you have to do is say something like, "Hey, your mom and I are going to get busy tonight."

They'll be so mortified they won't come near your bedroom! In fact, they'll probably call their friends and see if they can spend the night there.

Committing to seven days of sex will be fun, and it can encourage you to become creative and innovative, sensitive, giving, and forgiving. But most important, going through all of this for a week will help you understand the vital significance of sex in marriage.

Our culture has devalued sex into something that people do just because it feels good, like drinking cold lemonade on a hot day. Sex in marriage is so much more than something to do to fill a need. It's the superglue that bonds the marriage as you grow in oneness.

With that in mind, I encourage you to do it! Do it in marriage. Do it intentionally. Do it regularly. Do it enthusiastically. Do it creatively. Do it unselfishly. Do it, and God will bless your marriage and empower you to grow in oneness as you never imagined possible.

Action Steps

1. Review the seven outcomes of the Sexperiment and consider how they will help you and your spouse grow in oneness in your marriage.

2. Discuss with your spouse what high-definition marriage looks like in your relationship. Draft a blueprint of marriage in HD for you and your spouse.

3. Sincerely pray and ask God, "Lord, change me." Think about the ways you may need to be changed. Write them down as you pray and see how God uses your prayer to work in you and through you to strengthen your marriage.

4. Read the Song of Solomon in the Bible. As you get romantically inspired, write down some ideas that will keep your lovemaking innovative and creative during your Sexperiment week.

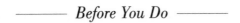

——— *Before You Do* ———

*O*neness doesn't just happen because you have a wedding or because you live under the same roof. Becoming one is a process that is an expression of a husband and wife's covenant with God and their covenant with each other. It's a gift that you give to the marriage and to each other.

There's no course you can take, no training DVD to watch or book to read to help you learn oneness in marriage. It's a life course that you can only learn by going through it. But having the right attitude about it helps.

Before you say "I do," cross-examine yourself. Are you going into the marriage with your own motives? Do you already have a plan in mind of how to change your future spouse? Have you decided that you will not give up certain attitudes or behaviors after you marry?

This kind of thinking and selfish agenda can kill any hope you have of becoming one. Strive to become one, because God designed it to be that way. Look at yourself and ask God to change you, so that you can have the right attitude going into the marriage.

Above all, consider the covenant relationship that God has with us. The Bible tells us there is nothing we can do to separate ourselves from God's love through Jesus Christ.*

That's the kind of commitment God wants us to model in marriage as we grow in becoming one.

The Yoke Is Not a Joke

A lot of single people, even Christians, believe they should have sex before marriage so that they'll know whether they're sexually compatible. They think it will help them solidify the relationship and build oneness as a couple.

Enjoying sex together is nothing like the coming together of a husband and wife under the protection of

---

* Romans 8:38–39

covenant marriage. These couples know that becoming one means a lot more than having sex, or living together or sharing household expenses.

Becoming one does include those things, but it begins with submitting to the covenant they made with God and with each other. Single people don't have that.

Very often singles think, "Hey, this feels pretty good. We get along so maybe we need to take it to the next level and have sex, or move in together." That's definitely not the next level! The next level is engagement—a time of reflection, preparation, and planning for a future life together as husband and wife.

Cohabitation and sex before marriage is not like trying on a pair of shoes to see if they fit. You may get a fit as a man and woman sharing the same household and the same bed, but it's no barometer as to whether the two of you can build oneness as a husband and wife. This is evidenced by the fact that the divorce rate is the same, if not higher, for those who live together before marriage as it is for those who don't. Sexual compatibility is one of those areas in which you have to grow together in oneness just like in the other areas of marriage.

It's amazing that single people are willing to have sex with a companion but would never go into debt with him or her without being married. But what's the greater risk, the greater loss?

Use the same caution and discretion about sex as you do about credit or finance. Giving your body away to someone can cost you so much more than going into debt together to buy a car.

Trust God to lead you to the right spouse, and then trust Him to guide you both toward oneness, which includes sexual compatibility.